Snowboarding

HEATHER E. SCHWARTZ

LUCENT BOOKS
A part of Gale, Cengage Learning

GALE
CENGAGE Learning™

Detroit • New York • San Francisco • New Haven, Conn • Waterville, Maine • London

LIBRARY OF CONGRESS CATALOGING-IN-PUBLICATION DATA

Schwartz, Heather E.
  Snowboarding / by Heather E. Schwartz.
    p. cm. — (The science behind sports)
  Includes bibliographical references and index.
  ISBN 978-1-4205-0322-7 (hardcover)
  1. Snowboarding. I. Title.
  GV857.S57S347 2011
  796.939—dc22
                                        2010033274

Lucent Books
27500 Drake Rd
Farmington Hills MI 48331

ISBN-13: 978-1-4205-0322-7
ISBN-10: 1-4205-0322-7

Printed in the United States of America
2 3 4 5 6 7 15 14 13 12 11

TABLE OF CONTENTS

FOREWORD

On March 21, 1970, Slovenian ski jumper Vinko Bogataj took a terrible fall while competing at the Ski-flying World Championships in Oberstdorf, West Germany. Bogataj's pinwheeling crash was caught on tape by an ABC *Wide World of Sports* film crew and eventually became synonymous with "the agony of defeat" in competitive sporting. While many viewers were transfixed by the severity of Bogataj's accident, most were not aware of the biomechanical and environmental elements behind the skier's fall—heavy snow and wind conditions that made the ramp too fast and Bogataj's inability to maintain his center of gravity and slow himself down. Bogataj's accident illustrates that, no matter how mentally and physically prepared an athlete may be, scientific principles—such as momentum, gravity, friction, and aerodynamics—always have an impact on performance.

Lucent Books' Science Behind Sports series explores these and many more scientific principles behind some of the most popular team and individual sports, including baseball, hockey, gymnastics, wrestling, swimming, and skiing. Each volume in the series focuses on one sport or group of related sports. The volumes open with a brief look at the featured sport's origins, history and changes, then move on to cover the biomechanics and physiology of playing, related health and medical concerns, and the causes and treatment of sports-related injuries.

In addition to learning about the arc behind a curve ball, the impact of centripetal force on a figure skater, or how water buoyancy helps swimmers, Science Behind Sports readers will also learn how exercise, training, warming up, and diet and nutrition directly relate to peak performance and enjoyment of the sport. Volumes may also cover why certain sports are popular, how sports function in the business world, and which hot sporting issues—sports doping and cheating, for example—are in the news.

Basic physical science concepts, such as acceleration, kinetics, torque, and velocity, are explained in an engaging and accessible manner. The full-color text is augmented by fact boxes, sidebars, photos, and detailed diagrams, charts and graphs. In addition, a subject-specific glossary, bibliography and index provide further tools for researching the sports and concepts discussed throughout Science Behind Sports.

CHAPTER 1

The Evolution of Snowboarding as a Sport

Snowboarding was once considered a sport for daredevils, rebels, and risk takers. After all, snowboarders, also called riders, do take risks. Their sport is performed by standing on a flat board and sliding down a mountain slope. Using the edge of the board, they slice through snow and ice, a process called carving in snowboarding. They also perform tricks by spinning, jumping, and flipping through the air.

"Since first strapping on their bindings in the early 1980s, snowboarders have gotten a bad rap for being aggressive and outlandish with their baggy clothes and irreverent attitudes," writes journalist Patrick Sweeney. "Many longtime skiers also complained that snowboarders compromise safety in favor of show-boating tricks."[1]

As the sport has evolved, however, accomplished snowboarders, like Shaun White, Peter Line, Hannah Teter, and Kelly Clark, have proven snowboarders have more control over their movements than some spectators might imagine. These athletes put scientific principles to work to maintain balance, regulate speed, control jumps, and land with precision. Whether they fully understand the physics behind the sport or not, science helps snowboarders train successfully,

perform competitively, manage risks, and avoid injury to themselves and others. They may look like daredevils on the hill, but in reality, they are serious and capable athletes.

Early Equipment

Snowboarding was not always known as a graceful and stylish sport. In fact, it began simply as a fun pastime. Even professional snowboarders have been surprised to learn how far back the history of snowboarding extends.

"I always thought snowboarding was a relatively new sport, but on a recent trip to Turkey, I realized it's actually been around for hundreds of years,"[2] professional snowboarder Jeremy Jones wrote on his blog after his trip in 2008.

In Turkey, Jones learned to ride a Turkish *lazboard,* a flat wooden board with a rope tied to one end. Riders hold the rope in one hand and a long stick in the other. Both are used for steering and balance. It is similar to a method early riders used in the United States.

Snowboarders control their movement by carving though snow and ice, utilizing the edge of their board.

"In the 1930s, kids experimented with standing up on their toboggans, holding onto the towrope for balance.… Turks think their *lazboard* has been around for 400 years, having been invented around 1600," writes journalist John Fry. "None of these early toboggan-like devices produces the modern snowboard's exotic sensation of banking against the centrifugal force of the turn, feet extended laterally, with nothing between your upper body and the snow. That happened in the 1980s."[3]

First, came the forerunners of modern snowboard design. In 1929 M.J. "Jack" Burchett designed one of the earliest snowboards similar to those used today. Unlike modern snowboards, which are made of a combination of wood, fiberglass, and plastic, it was made of plywood. It lacked metal edges to carve into the snow. It was also missing bindings to attach the rider's boots to the board. Burchett secured himself to the board by tying his feet with clothesline and horse reins.

The next leap in snowboard development did not occur until 1965, when engineer Sherman Poppen invented a toy for his daughters. Taking advantage of ski technology, which was already further along, Poppen created a snowboard made of two skis tied together with a rope for the rider to hold. His wife, Nancy, named it the Snurfer, because it allowed riders to combine snow with surfing.

Rebel Riders Compete

In 1990 the newly established United States Amateur Snowboarding Association (USASA) held its first national championship event, at Snow Valley, in California. When a snowstorm hit, the snowboarders lived up to their rebellious reputation. Roads leading to the event were closed, so USASA founder Chuck Allen, a former Snurf coach, decided to get around the rules. He sneaked snowboarders past police barricades, so they could compete. Since then, the USASA has held national championships annually for snowboarders.

Evolving Equipment

After licensing his idea to a manufacturer, Poppen began organizing Snurfer competitions for kids. By the mid-1960s, snowboarding was taking off and gaining recognition as more than a winter pastime. Poppen's competitions even drew a serious skier whose name is now famous in the snowboarding industry.

Jake Burton had broken his collarbone and could not compete as a skier anymore. He took up competing on the Snurfer instead.

"The minute I got on a Snurfer and rode it, I knew there was a sport there. The early Snurfers had no bindings, edges or P-Tex bases, but when you got on them in powder you could definitely shred," Burton says. "From that point on I always talked about the idea of starting a real snowboarding company and making it a sport."[4]

The Snurfer was closer to today's snowboard than earlier designs. Without bindings, however, the Snurfer was less energy efficient than modern snowboards. The energy transfer from the rider's boots to the board was not as direct, because the rider needed some energy to stay on the board. The lack of metal edges meant that maintaining control on snow and ice was difficult. The board could easily skid and slip. Also, the Snurfer did not have a coating of P-Tex, a polyurethane material, on its base, or underside. That made the board slower, because it was more likely to create friction as it moved through the snow. Friction is created when two objects rub against one another and causes resistance to forward motion.

SHREDDING AND STOMPING

5.1 million

Number of snowboarders that hit the slopes in 2001, according to the National Ski and Snowboard Retailers Association.

Burton's Board

Burton liked the Snurfer, but he thought he could improve on the design. After he graduated from college in 1977, he got to work. He made one hundred prototypes before settling on a design. "They were all made of entirely different constructions, from marine plywood, to fiberglass, to solid ash that I steamed and bent as if making a chair,"[5] he says.

Former skier Jake Burton improved the design of Sherman Popper's Snurfer—an early version of the snowboard—by adding metal edges and developing bindings to secure the rider's feet.

In the end, he developed a new kind of snowboard with bindings to secure the riders' feet to the board. Later, Burton made further improvements by adding metal edges to his design and creating a plastic base for better gliding with less friction.

When Burton began manufacturing his boards, he changed the sport of snowboarding forever. He proved that using bindings made a major difference in how the sport was performed. The energy transfer from boots to board was

THE PARTS OF A SNOWBOARD

TOP   BASE

Nose Length

Nose Width

Effective Edge

The unique design of a snowboard enables a rider to remain in control on the slopes.

Waist Width

Overall Length

Flex Point

Sidecut Radius

Stomping Pad

Binding Holes

Tail Width

Tail Length

Contact Point

Camber

Contact Point

much more direct because extra energy was not required to stay on the board. The board reacted more quickly to shifts of body mass and positioning, giving riders more control on the hill.

Snowboarding on the Slopes

Burton's new design worked, but it was difficult for anyone to test it out on a big mountain. Like those who rode Snurfers, people who wanted to try Burton's new design had to hike up a hill on a golf course or in a sledding area. Most mountain resorts would not permit snowboarders, including Snurfers, to ride. Resort operators were concerned that snowboarders would not have control on the slopes. "They would tell us they'd never seen [a snowboard] before and didn't want us on their hill,"[6] Burton says.

In 1985, 93 percent of ski resorts banned snowboarding. Burton helped change that slowly over time. He went on to found Burton Snowboards, which manufactures snowboards, boots, bindings, outerwear, goggles, and other equipment.

"He persevered, becoming a one-man cheerleading squad for the sport. He visited hundreds of ski hills that had banned snowboarding, trying to coax reluctant resort owners into allowing it," writes journalist Bruce Horovitz. "Many equated snowboarding with rowdiness, or worse. But one by one, they relented."[7]

Because they were often self-taught, snowboarders were sometimes required to take a skills assessment test to prove they were capable of staying in control and would not crash into skiers or each other. Organizations such as the Southwest Snow Surfing Association certified instructors for this task. "The idea was to have instructors teach and then verify that riders could turn, slow down and stop before they were allowed to go up on the mountain,"[8] explains Randy Price, an American Association of Snowboard Instructors (AASI) level 3 instructor, team alum, and past AASI team coach.

Snowboarders also found themselves segregated from skiers at some resorts. They could ride only on slopes specifically designated for snowboarders.

Snowboard Pioneers

In addition to Jake Burton, other early snowboard designers included Demetrije Milovich, Tom Sims, and Bev and Chris Sanders. Milovich worked with a surfboard shaper in the late 1960s to create his design. He later founded Winterstick Snowboards in 1976.

Tom Sims designed his snowboard based on skateboard designs. He attached carpet to the top of the board and aluminum sheeting to the base. He founded Sims Snowboards, also in 1976.

Bev and Chris Sanders started out making snowboards for their own use. People kept asking about them and buying the boards, so they founded Avalanche Snowboards in 1982.

Snowboarders were easy to spot at ski resorts. Not only did they use different equipment than skiers, they also stood out as mainly teenagers wearing signature baggy clothing. They were stereotyped as rebellious, undisciplined, and even rude.

While they were considered risk takers, snowboarders were also enthusiastic. This attitude helped them continue developing the sport as new technology and snowboarding equipment continued to advance.

Equipment Advances

Snowboarding technology has come a long way since M.J. Burchett made his plywood board back in 1929. Today's snowboards are made of several layers of different materials. The core is usually made of wood or a combination of composite materials. It is designed to be lightweight, strong, and flexible.

Fiberglass is layered on top of the core to reinforce strength. Next comes the topsheet, a layer of plastic that protects the board's inner materials. The topsheet is often decorated with graphics that make each board unique.

The bottom of the board is layered with P-Tex, a brand of polyurethane material. It is slippery and helps the board glide better and overcome friction, a force that could slow the board down. Friction is resistance to motion that is created when two objects, such as the board and the snow, rub together. This rubbing transforms some of the kinetic energy, which is the energy of motion required to move the board, into heat and sound instead. As a result, the board loses speed.

Modern snowboards are curved to aid riders as they create their turn shapes. They are wider at the edges with a narrower sidecut, or middle section. The edges of the board are lined with steel, so the snowboarder can carve more easily into hard-packed snow and ice.

Modern snowboarding boots are also designed with technology to aid the rider. Snowboarders used to wear work boots or even basketball sneakers, which would be soaked after a few runs. Today's boots are lined with foam to cushion, support, and keep feet warm. The outer shell is generally made of synthetic leather or hard plastic material that will prevent water from seeping in.

Snowboarding Styles

Without the latest equipment, modern snowboarding would not be possible. Today's snowboarders perform in several different disciplines, including racing, freestyle, and all-mountain snowboarding, which are showcased in competitions that include events such as half-pipe, superpipe, snowboardcross, alpine, and slopestyle. Each event is defined by specific skills and requirements, and each puts science to work in a different way.

In half-pipe events, individual snowboarders perform tricks on snow that has been carved into a curved shape. "Half-pipe is a sport that relies heavily on physics and the complex interplay between speed, gravity and balance," writes Greg Wells, a scientist specializing in extreme human physiology. "Snowboarders build up speed every way they can—trying to pick the best line down the pipe, pumping their legs, and then holding their core stable and strong as

they fly up the wall of the half-pipe."[9] The line is the path a snowboarder decides to follow or create.

Superpipe is similar to half-pipe, but on a larger scale. Half-pipes are less than 18 feet (5.5m) tall and 25 feet (7.6m) wide. Superpipes are at least that large, or larger. In superpipes, snowboarders can use the larger walls to gain more height in the air when performing tricks such as spins, grabs, and hand plants.

Snowboardcross and alpine snowboarding are races that pit riders against one another. In these disciplines, speed and control are critical. In snowboardcross, snowboarders race through gates set up on the course. The gates, which look like two short colored posts holding a square of material between them, mark the fastest path down the hill. In alpine snowboarding, the riders contend with jumps and ramps along the course.

When they are racing, snowboarders put Sir Isaac Newton's first law of motion into action. Newton, a mathematician and physicist of the late seventeenth and early eighteenth centuries,

Halfpipes—snow that has been carved into a curved shape—allow individual snowboarders to perform spins, grabs, and other tricks.

The Evolution of Snowboarding as a Sport 15

SHREDDING AND STOMPING

1988

The year the United States Amateur Snowboarding Association (USASA) was incorporated to standardize national rules for snowboard competitions. It is now called the United States of America Snowboard Association.

developed the first law of motion when he discovered that an object in motion stays in motion unless it is stopped by another force. In races, snowboarders gain momentum, a force that keeps them moving in the same direction with more and more speed. It can be calculated by multiplying a snowboarder's body mass and velocity, or speed.

Momentum can also work against snowboarders, however, if they fail to stay in control of their movements. Even when racing, snowboarders need to control turns so they do not skid out and hit jumps precisely so they do not crash. "When racing, snowboarders control their turn shape to keep themselves on line and to hit jumps precisely; a clean line maximizes speed and the potential for a crash-free landing,"[10] Price explains.

Slopestyle snowboarding tests a rider's freestyle skills on a course full of features, or special challenges built into the snow. Features can be made of snow as well as other objects. Snowboarders use the obstacles to perform tricks, such as a rail slide. In a rail slide, the board slides along an object, like the edge of a ramp, that is not made of snow. To perform the trick, snowboarders need to gain momentum, jump up onto the object, and maintain balance while their speed changes. At the end of the rail, the rider must hop off the rail, land, and keep moving, without falling or crashing.

Snowboarders Gain Respect

In 1997 snowboarding events were part of the Winter X Games, a national competition. Many believe snowboarding was fully legitimized when riders competed in the Olympic Games for the first time in 1998. They competed in half-pipe and individual giant slalom, an alpine race. Today, Olympic snowboarders compete in half-pipe events, alpine races, and snowboardcross.

Sweeney writes:

Call it the old school vs. the new school or the brash upstarts vs. the traditional establishment. Whatever you call it, there is an undeniable rivalry between snowboarders and skiers. But like a younger sibling who was once considered rebellious and bratty in younger days, snowboarding has seen its legitimacy grow as it matures into an acceptable mainstream sport. And the sport is showing no signs of going away. Many ski industry insiders cite the sport's Winter Olympics debut in 1998 in Nagano, Japan, for giving the younger-skewing sport a sense of legitimacy.[11]

By the 2010 Olympic Games in Vancouver, Canada, snowboarders were still showing some of the attitude that once shocked those outside the sport. They popped in earbuds and listened to their own music during events. That helped them block out other sounds and get pumped up to familiar tunes. They wore their signature baggy outfits that some critics have complained hinder speed. Tighter-fitting clothing would create a more aerodynamic shape with less surface area meeting with air molecules and causing friction during motion.

Despite anyone's concerns about attitude or fashion, the U.S. Snowboarding Team did well at the 2010 Olympic Games. They took gold medals in men's half-pipe and men's snowboardcross. Spectators were most impressed with snowboarder Shaun White's gold medal execution of a move called the Double McTwist 1260, which involved two backflips and three and a half full rotations in the air.

"Shaun White literally soared above his competition in the men's half-pipe event at Cypress Mountain, British Columbia ..., delivering the U.S. its fifth gold medal in 2010, and sealing the snowboarder's legacy as one of the most dominant Olympians in history,"[12] wrote journalist Reed Albergotti at the time of the competition.

In addition, the U.S. team took a silver in ladies' half-pipe and bronze in ladies' and men's half-pipe. At the 2010 Olympics, top snowboarders proved that, image aside, these athletes know how to harness scientific forces that can help them perform their best and win the highest honors in their sport.

CHAPTER 2

Training and Conditioning for Snowboarding

S nowboarding is a sport that puts riders on flat terrain, gentle slopes, and steep pitches. Riders may find themselves trying to carve a turn or perform a trick in powder, slush, or ice. Terrain conditions can vary from day to day, hour to hour, and even within minutes due to changes in the weather. At every moment, riders tune in to the scientific forces around them to gain control, precision, and power on the hill.

In order to work with those forces and compensate for changing conditions, snowboarders use a great deal of muscle strength, especially in their lower body. While they need to train and condition to build that strength, snowboarders traditionally have not taken such steps.

According to Olympic snowboarder Gretchen Bleiler, "When I first started snowboarding, nobody trained off-hill. People weren't going to the gym and getting stronger. Snowboarding was more self-expression, like skateboarding. It was just something you went and did. It wasn't something you trained for."[13]

Training intensity changed when people began to view snowboarding as a competitive sport. Burton won his first

Training Early

Elite snowboarders start training at an early age to make it to the top in their sport. Olympic snowboarder Shaun White first tried snowboarding at age six. Olympic snowboarder Kelly Clark got into the sport as a third grader. Olympic snowboarder Lindsey Jacobellis began snowboarding at nine and was competing by age eleven. Starting young gives snowboarders an edge in competition because they have had years of practice. They may also be less fearful of trying tricks and handling speed.

At the same time, young competitive snowboarders sometimes miss out on normal activities in order to follow their dreams. In the November 5, 2009, *Teen Vogue,* Jacobellis spoke about growing up to be an elite athlete:

You just have to be sure you really truly love it. You'll have to give up certain things to get ahead. You have to lose something to gain something. I didn't go to a normal high school, or get to do a lot of things that other kids were doing, all for the sport. So the most important thing is just to be really, really sure you love the sport otherwise it won't feel worth it.

Source: Laurel Pantin. Teen Vogue. Chatting with Olympic Snowboarder Lindsey Jacobellis. November 5, 2009.

http://www.teenvogue.com/beauty/blogs/beauty/2009/11/chatting-with-olympic-snowboarder-lindsey-jacobellis.html.

race on a snowboard in a Snurfer competition in 1979. Just a few years later, in 1982, the first National Snowboard race was held at Suicide Six, a resort near Woodstock, Vermont. With snowboarding officially evolving into more than a laid-back winter pastime, snowboarders began to put more thought into the science at work in their sport.

Warming Up

While snowboarding is definitely a good workout in itself, riding to get fit only makes the sport more difficult. Snowboarders need to work out off the slopes, too, so their bodies will be prepared ahead of time to perform. Serious snowboarders warm up before they hit the hill. They also warm up before other kinds of training and conditioning that can prepare them for snowboarding.

Riders often warm up with activities that increase the heart rate, like lunges, when working out off the slopes.

In order to warm up, snowboarders do activities like deep lunges, walking uphill, and jumping, which cause the heart rate to increase. When the heart pumps faster, it delivers more blood at a faster rate to muscles throughout the circulatory system, which in turn moves blood throughout the entire body. Breathing rate also increases during the warm-up, pulling more oxygen into the snowboarder's lungs. This oxygen is delivered into the circulatory system through alveoli, tiny sacs within the lungs.

When muscles are warmed up, they are filled with blood that carries both nutrients and oxygen. The blood literally raises the temperature of the muscles, which also relaxes stretch reflexes. As a result, the warmed-up muscle tissue will stretch more easily and without tearing compared to cold muscle tissue.

Warming up not only benefits muscles, but also stimulates production of synovial fluid, a lubricant between joints, and warms the fluid, so it is less viscous, or thick and sticky. When synovial fluid flows, it eases friction caused when joints rub together during movement. Synovial fluid makes it easier to move joints, and it prevents pain.

In fact, warming up can prepare the entire nervous system, which includes the brain, spinal cord, and nerves, for working out or snowboarding. By the end of a warm-up session, neurons, which transmit nerve impulses, can send messages faster from the brain and spinal reflex center to muscles. As a result, riders will be able to react quickly to physical challenges, whether working out in the gym or snowboarding down a slope.

"I love my warm-up, actually, because it gets all of my muscles ready and firing," Olympic snowboarder Kelly Clark says. "It's simple squats, non-weight-bearing, and they get my quads and glutes ready for the day."[14]

Snowboarding Takes Strength

Once the body is sufficiently warmed up, snowboarders are ready for a more intense workout. The purpose of working out is to build strength, particularly in the rider's leg muscles. These muscles include the quadriceps, hamstrings, abductors, adductors, and the gluteal muscles. Snowboarders also use their lower-back muscles, abdominal muscles, triceps, and latissimus dorsi. Plus, they need strong core muscles, which include abdominals and other muscles that stabilize the torso between the shoulders and pelvis along the spine.

According to Bleiler, muscle strength can benefit a snowboarder in many different ways. "You have to be strong, and you have to know how to use your body properly and how to fire the correct muscles. All of these things are great for

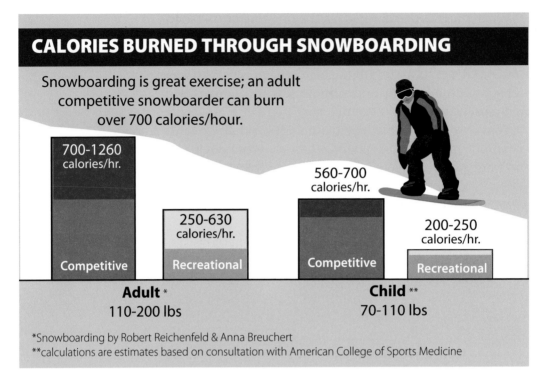

CALORIES BURNED THROUGH SNOWBOARDING

Snowboarding is great exercise; an adult competitive snowboarder can burn over 700 calories/hour.

700-1260 calories/hr.

560-700 calories/hr.

250-630 calories/hr.

200-250 calories/hr.

Competitive

Recreational

Competitive

Recreational

Adult *
110-200 lbs

Child **
70-110 lbs

*Snowboarding by Robert Reichenfeld & Anna Breuchert
**calculations are estimates based on consultation with American College of Sports Medicine

injury prevention. Not just that, but also confidence. When you're up on the hill and you know you're as strong as you can be, you're more willing and able and confident to go and do bigger and harder and more technical tricks,"[15] she says.

Snowboarders put their muscles to work during every moment they are on the slopes. While the force of gravity is pulling them down, they use their leg muscles to dig the edge of the board into the snow. They use their back muscles to twist their hips and carve turns that control speed and direction. When riders are in motion, they must always keep their center of gravity over the riding edge of the board to maintain balance. The riding edge is the edge that is engaged in the snow. It switches as riders make their turns. The center of gravity is the point of balance in a snowboarder's body where forces act equally on all sides. For example, gravity pulls down at the center of gravity, but the snowboarder pushes up with the same amount of force in order to stay balanced and upright.

Snowboarders also use their leg, back, and core muscles during landings. On impact, landing forces are created when a snowboarder hits the snow from a height. For example, when performing tricks such as flips and spins, snowboarders often launch high into the air. When Shaun White performed his Double McTwist 1260, he went about 20 feet (6m) above the half-pipe. U.S. Snowboarding Team coach Rick Bower commented to the media afterward on White's strength as a snowboarder.

"He's using a lot of his core muscles. He definitely has a lot of strength in his legs and back muscles. He's wiry-strong, and definitely in shape,"[16] he said.

The higher snowboarders fly in the air, the greater the impact will be upon landing. As riders fall back to the ground, gravitational acceleration causes them to fall increasingly faster. Their muscles help them absorb the landing forces and maintain balance and stability to continue performing.

Working Out

In order to develop the muscle strength they need, snowboarders do both aerobic and anaerobic exercises off the hill. Activities like walking, jogging, and cycling are considered aerobic exercises because they increase the body's need for oxygen in the blood to fuel muscles. Aerobic exercise strengthens the cardiovascular system, or circulatory system, made up of the heart, blood, and blood vessels. It also builds slow-twitch muscle fibers, which help snowboarders with endurance, or stamina. Slow-twitch muscles do not tire as quickly as fast-twitch muscles, since they contract more slowly.

Anaerobic exercises are also part of a serious rider's workout. During anaerobic exercise, muscles are fueled by glucose rather than oxygen. This kind of exercise develops fast-twitch muscle fiber, which contracts quickly, creating intense bursts of explosive energy. Snowboarders use their robust fast-twitch muscles to defy gravity and punch up into the air off a ramp or the half-pipe.

Snowboarders who want to build fast-twitch muscles do plyometrics, a system of exercises—such as jumps and throws—that stretch muscles and contract them forcefully, stimulating muscles to grow. They also practice sprints, train

Snowboarders do aerobic exercises such as jogging in order to develop muscle strength.

with increasingly heavy weights, and do interval training, which alternates high-intensity exercise with periods of rest. By challenging muscles until they are fatigued, snowboarders actually tear the tissue slightly. That stimulates new cells to repair the tissue. The new cells create thicker, stronger muscle fibers overall.

Regarding his workout, White says:

I'm not trying to build up muscle or bulk, or anything like that. In a lot of traditional sports you need to be big—you need to knock over someone who's bigger than you. But it's a different strength you're looking for in snowboarding. It's more like tennis. You gotta be quick and you've gotta be really mentally prepared. You gotta predict where you're gonna go, where you're going to land, what you're going to see."[17]

Stretching and Balancing

Riders round out their workouts with stretching and balancing exercises. Stretching helps them gain range of motion in joints and flexibility in muscles, which is especially needed in their quadriceps and hamstrings. Greater range of motion and flexibility make riders less prone to injury due to over-extension or torn tissue.

Static stretches are performed by holding a stretch, such as a lunge. Dynamic stretches are performed by incorporating motion into the stretch. For example, a rider may perform walking lunges. While serious riders are more likely to do stretches than occasional snowboarders, riders at every level can be seen doing stretches on the lift line.

Balancing exercises teach riders to keep their center of gravity over their base of support while standing still as well as in motion. Static exercises involve standing on one leg while moving the other. Riders may also practice staying in balance while hopping forward and backward. Putting their arms out to the sides can help riders stay balanced. This stance redistributes body mass so the force of gravity is not concentrated at one point.

White has talked about the importance of working out to improve balance:

> When you're losing balance on your snowboard—doing that arm waving thing—, what you're doing is straining yourself, and your body is grabbing every single muscle around it in order to bring you back into balance. So, that's what you're trying to do. You're trying to strengthen all those little muscles that help the big muscles, and build overall strength—not size.[18]

SHREDDING AND STOMPING

24

The number of hours per week that snowboarders in top half-pipe competitions train.

Honing Snowboarding Skills Year-Round

Training and conditioning for snowboarding does not always mean just going to the gym. Many elite snowboarders travel to make sure they can ride on snow throughout the year. "Training for top snowboarders has evolved into a year-round global pursuit, complete with summer sessions on glaciers or in the Southern Hemisphere,"[19] writes journalist Matt Higgins.

Adam Moran, global team manager for Burton Snowboards, has also commented that top snowboarders cannot

Many snowboarders are active in complementary sports as a way of cross-training. Professional snowboarder Shaun White also performs as a professional skateboarder which helps him to maintain his body control.

afford to take summers off when they are training. "Nowadays, if you're a top competitive snowboarder, riding all summer long is pretty much a necessity. There are a lot of contests in December each year, and if riders don't get on snow this summer, they will only have a month or so to get everything back from the winter before, which can be tough,"[20] he says.

While not all snowboarders can travel to train on the slopes, many are active in summer sports that use similar skills and work the same muscles as snowboarding. While recovering from an injury in spring 2008, Olympic snowboarder Graham Watanabe spent about five days a week at a training center. "During the season, you're focusing on equipment, sleep and downtime, but this is when we work the hardest," he says. "I put a majority of my work in during the off season. It's an oxymoron—off season. The off season is when we winter athletes work the hardest."[21]

Snowboarders have also been known to benefit from pursuing complementary sports, also called cross-training. Kelly Clark surfs and bikes during the summer. Like snowboarding, surfing requires athletes to balance on a board and ride the changing terrain. Biking is also good training for balance as well as for conditioning muscles and building endurance.

"I enjoy doing other sports: I got into mountain biking, and I love surfing if I can get to the beach anywhere. In surfing, if you can figure out how the ocean works once you're standing up, it's very similar to snowboarding. I started surfing when I was about 12, because I enjoyed snowboarding so much,"[22] she says.

According to Gretchen Bleiler, using the trampoline is another good conditioning activity. "Jumping on the trampoline for even a half an hour is a really good workout. You get really tired. The next day you're feeling it. And you really have to use your core. If you don't, your lower back hurts the next day,"[23] she says.

White is a professional skateboarder as well as a professional snowboarder. Skateboarding also requires movements that are similar to snowboarding. "Skateboarding really helps me stay fresh. The technique is different because your feet aren't attached to the board, but both sports are about controlling your body in space, finding a feeling for the trick,"[24] he says.

Whether snowboarding or participating in other sports activities, finding a way to practice is essential for snowboarders who want to improve their skills. Repeating skills over and over gets both the muscles and the brain accustomed to performing specific movements. At first, a snowboarder has to consciously think about each move, which requires energy and concentration. Eventually, with enough practice, the required moves are controlled by the cerebellum, the part of the brain that controls unconscious movement.

Cooling Down

Serious snowboarders do not limit their training and conditioning to warming up, working out, and riding. They also need to think about cooling down after they work out as well as after they ride. When challenging exercise is stopped abruptly, blood pools and muscles tend to swell and tighten.

Cooling down means that exercise is stopped more gradually to prevent that discomfort. After a workout, snowboarders

Special Diet

Some snowboarders follow more restrictive diets than others for personal reasons. As long as they get the nutrients they need, they can perform to the top of their abilities. Olympic snowboarder Hannah Teter, for example, became a vegetarian as an elite athlete. Her protein comes from foods like quinoa (a grain) rather than meat. In a February 23, 2010, *Sports Illustrated* interview Teter explained:

There are so many different ways to get protein as a vegetarian, like Warrior Protein, which is all these different raw sprouted grains—it's higher protein than meat and better for you. After I became a vegetarian about a year ago, I felt so much different, and way more clear, but I was sore for a couple of days, because the buildup of the fatty acids from the meat has to come out of your body.

Source: Luke Winn. "Q&A with U.S. Snowboarder Hannah Teter." SI.com. February 23, 2010. http://sportsillustrated. cnn.com/olympics/2010/blog/2010/02/23/qa-with-u-s-snowboarder-hannah-teter/.

may ride a stationary bike, stretch, or do yoga. After intense snowboarding, riders often cool down by riding less aggressively on a long trail with less challenging terrain. These types of activities can help hasten circulation and move oxygen and nutrients through the blood to repair muscles, tendons, and ligaments that have been torn or damaged during a workout or while on the hill.

Eating Right

In addition to working out, snowboarders have to prepare their bodies for their sport by eating a nutritious diet tailored to accommodate their active lifestyle. Before heading out on the hill, snowboarders are advised to eat complex carbohydrates, such as oatmeal, rice, granola, and bread. These kinds of foods create the enduring energy they will need to perform. When digested, carbohydrates break down and create sugars like glycogen that feed fast-twitch muscle fibers. Complex carbohydrates break down more slowly than simple carbohydrates, which are likely to create a burst of energy followed by an energy crash.

Protein is an important part of a snowboarder's diet, too, though not necessarily during the hour before going out to ride. Proteins, found in foods like chicken and fish, are broken down into amino acids during digestion. Amino acids rebuild muscle tissue so snowboarders will stay strong after a hard workout or performance.

Snowboarders need enduring energy in order to perform their complex tricks, and as a result are advised to eat complex carbohydrates, such as oatmeal, rice, granola, and bread.

SHREDDING AND STOMPING

75 percent
Amount of muscle tissue made of water.

"I find that as long as I'm eating enough, I'm OK. I just have to make sure I'm getting enough calories and a lot of protein. I'm always having snack bars and power shakes when we're on the hill so I can make it until lunch!"[25] Clark says.

Staying Hydrated

One thing no snowboarder can do without is drinking fluids to prevent dehydration. Muscle tissue needs fluid to function. When snowboarders are cold, they do not always recognize they are thirsty. Also, by the time they feel thirsty, they will already be dehydrated. For that reason, snowboarders need to make sure they stay hydrated regardless of whether they feel thirsty. Dehydration can cause dizziness, raise heart rate, upset body temperature, and impair mental functioning.

Snowboarders generally drink water or sports drinks before and while riding. Before the 2010 Olympic Games, Olympic snowboarder Lindsey Jacobellis blogged for Health .com about eating right and staying hydrated while preparing for competition.

"Leading up to an event, I am …very careful to stay as healthy as possible," she wrote. "Usually I just follow typical mom advice of eating nutritious foods, exercising, and drinking lots of water, and it seems to work. Plus, I have a secret weapon for hydration—coconut water!"[26]

While coconut water can help snowboarders stay hydrated, it has the added benefit of preventing cramps. Coconut water has fifteen times the potassium found in most sports drinks. Potassium is a mineral that aids muscle growth, muscle contractions and nerve-cell function. Without enough potassium, which can be lost through sweating, muscles tend to cramp. When snowboarders train, condition, eat right, and stay hydrated, however, they are prepared to meet physical challenges and perform their best on the hill.

CHAPTER 3

Preparing for Snowboarding

S nowboarders use all sorts of equipment to maximize their performance and prevent injury. At the minimum, they need a pair of snowboarding boots and a snowboard in order to perform properly in this sport. While some riders may be tempted to choose boots based on look and boards based on graphics, serious athletes know that the right equipment can make a big difference in how they execute turns and perform tricks.

The Right Snowboarding Boots

During snowboarding, energy transfers through the rider's boots to the board. This transfer is made more efficient by using bindings that hold the boots in place. It is also made more efficient when riders choose boots that fit snugly. If boots are loose, they can cause the rider's feet to slip around inside. Extra energy will be needed to stay in balance on the board, which can cause muscles to cramp and fatigue. "Good boots will feel comfortable and bouncy if they're made right, not too stiff or too mushy,"[27] Olympic snowboarder Hannah Teter says.

Snowboarding boots come in different styles to match different types of riding. Riders who want to focus on tricks need extra-flexible boots that will bend at the ankles for

Snowboarding boots come in different styles to match the various riding techniques. Snowboarders who focus on tricks need flexibility in their boots.

jumps and flips. Riders who want to tackle all kinds of terrain need stiffer boots that provide more stability on steep slopes and hard-packed snow.

Choosing a Board

Snowboarders also have to consider riding style when they choose a board. They have to consider many other factors, too, including their height and the size of their feet. A board stood on end should reach between the rider's chin and nose. If it is longer it will be faster but more difficult to maneuver. The board should be wide enough so that the rider's feet do not hang off and drag, creating extra friction that will slow the board down. At the same time, it should not be more than an inch or two wider than the length of the rider's feet. If the board is too wide, the rider will not be able to put enough pressure on the edges for controlled turns.

Beginners usually start out with a wide basic freestyle board. Wide boards are more stable than narrow boards because they have more surface area on the snow. Basic freestyle boards are also about the same width at tip and tail.

The Science of Wax

Wax technicians are professionals who tune snowboards, which means maintaining a good sliding surface for snow conditions by applying wax to the base. Wax technicians measure the air temperature, the water content in the snow and the size of snow crystals to determine exactly how the wax should be applied for the best results. A good wax job can gain a rider seconds in races that are won by hundredths of a second.

As author K.C. Althen explains in *The Complete Book of Snowboarding,*

> The structure of snow varies with its age. New, sharply crystalline snow or snow that is very cold needs a harder wax to prevent the snow from physically gouging the wax, on a microscopic scale, which reduces the glide. Older snow has rounded edges, and warmed or sun-exposed snow requires a softer wax. Softer waxes lose less energy to friction.

Source: K.C. Althen, *The Complete Book of Snowboarding.* Charles E. Tuttle, Co., Inc. 1990. P. 114-115.

This design makes it easier to learn how to steer because whether leading with tail or tip, going downhill will always feel the same.

More advanced snowboarders often use freeride boards or alpine boards, also known as carving boards. Freeride boards are soft and easy to bend. They are stiffer than basic freestyle boards, however, so they are better for carving into hard snow and holding an edge on a steep slope despite the force of gravity pushing downward. Alpine boards are long, narrow and stiff. They are good for racing because they hold an edge without vibrating and remain stable at high speeds.

More About Boards

The sidecut of a board determines how comfortable a rider will be with wide and sharp turns. The sidecut gives the board its narrower shape at the center and affects the turning radius when a snowboarder is carving turns. Turning radius measures the shape of the sidecut based on a circle. A deeper sidecut has a smaller turning radius, so the board can make tighter turns. Straighter boards with less sidecut will have a larger turning radius. They are meant for speed and making wide turns.

Sidecut is not the only factor that determines how the board will turn. Flex, camber, and a rider's ability in the sport are all part of the equation. Flex measures how stiff or soft the board is. As a snowboarder rides down a slope, the board bends. Stiff boards are more stable in the snow, but they are only as effective as the rider using them. Because they require more energy to bend, they are best for aggressive, experienced riders and heavier riders. Softer boards are easier for beginners and lighter riders to use. At the same time, a soft board may vibrate, or chatter, if it is not stiff enough to keep an edge in the snow at high speeds.

Camber refers to the arch shape that is built into the board. When there is no weight on the board, camber causes the center to rise above the surface of the ground. When in use, the camber distributes the rider's weight to the tip, or front, and tail, or back, so it is not concentrated in the center. This more even distribution of weight makes the board more stable and easier to control.

Warm, Dry Clothing

Because snowboarding is a winter sport, riders need to dress properly for the weather. Many prefer warm, sunny days for snowboarding. Those who are serious about the sport, however, know it is just as important to get out there on cold, dark, windy days. They have to train, no matter what the conditions or how they are feeling. In order to endure winter weather without allowing it to hinder performance, riders dress to stay warm and dry, which can give them a psychological as well as a physical edge.

Snowboarders wear waterproof gloves with good grip. On especially cold days, they may put heat packs inside their gloves. Layers of clothing on their bodies keep them comfortable in changing weather conditions. The first layer must wick sweat away from the skin. New technology has allowed for the creation of man-made fabrics that can absorb moisture without feeling wet next to the skin, unlike natural fibers such as cotton or wool.

Fleece is an ideal middle layer of clothing. It is lightweight and holds warm air close to the rider's body. The outer layer of clothing must be roomy enough to allow the rider to move easily. Pants are often reinforced at the seat and knees where riders bend and fall. Both jacket and pants enhance the rider's experience if they are windproof, waterproof, and breathable. GORE-TEX®, for example, is a brand of fabric used in outerwear that is designed with pores twenty thousand times

Unusual Uniform

When members of the U.S. Snowboarding Team competed at the 2010 Olympic Games, they appeared to be wearing plaid jackets and worn jeans. Their pants were not really made of faded, torn denim, however. Instead, they were fashioned out of GORE-TEX®, a light, flexible, waterproof fabric ideal for outdoor sports. The design, by Burton Snowboards, was meant to help the athletes perform, provide a uniform look for the team, and also show a certain snowboarding style.

"This is snowboarding," said Greg Dacyshyn, creative director at Burton, as quoted in a December 7, 2009, blog on ESPN.com. "It's never been a uniform sport, so we wanted to create a look that would reflect those unique qualities of our sport, but still capture a classic American feel."

Source: Tracy Anderson, "2010 Olympic Snowboard (Anti) Uniforms," ESPN, December 7, 2009. http://espn.go.com/action/snowboarding/blog/_/post/4722162.

smaller than a water droplet. That makes it waterproof. At the same time, the pores are seven hundred times bigger than a water vapor molecule, so perspiration can evaporate through the material.

Protective Gear

Beyond keeping warm and dry, snowboarders also need gear that can protect them from the hazards on the slopes. Goggles help ensure good vision no matter what the weather conditions. Tinted styles are worn on sunny days, while clear styles are used on cloudy days or for night snowboarding. Goggles protect the rider's eyes from ultraviolet (UV) rays, wind, and obstacles they might encounter on a trail, such as ice and tree branches.

Besides protecting the eyes, riders need to protect their bodies. Beginners and riders learning new tricks often wear hip pads, which cushion the tailbone during a fall. They also wear knee pads, which allow the knees to bend but protect the joint from the impact of a fall. Wrist guards specifically designed for snow sports can help prevent wrist fractures. They are stiff and fit inside the rider's gloves.

At mountain resorts, riders must use a leash, a device that clips the binding to a boot to prevent a runaway board on the slope. And at every level, riders wear helmets. A helmet protects the rider's head in case of a collision with another rider,

Snowboarders need protective gear such as goggles, wrist guards, and gloves to shield them from the hazards of the slopes.

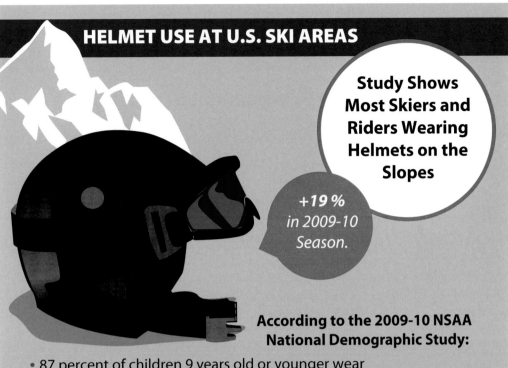

HELMET USE AT U.S. SKI AREAS

Study Shows Most Skiers and Riders Wearing Helmets on the Slopes

+19% in 2009-10 Season.

According to the 2009-10 NSAA National Demographic Study:

- 87 percent of children 9 years old or younger wear ski/snowboard helmets;

- 75 percent of children between 10 and 14 wear ski/snowboard helmets;

- 70 percent of adults over the age of 65 wear ski/snowboard helmets;

- Skiers and snowboarders aged 18 to 24 have traditionally represented the lowest percentage of helmet use among all age groups.

In 2009-10, 43 percent of all 18 to 24 year olds interviewed wore helmets, representing a 139 percent increase in usage for this age group since the 2002-03 season, when only 18 percent wore helmets.

the ground, or a tree. It also keeps the rider's head warm. Some are ventilated, so the rider will not become too hot. Most resorts do not require helmet use, but many are moving in that direction for safety reasons. According to a 2010 report by *ScienceDaily*, each year about 120,000 people in

North America sustain head injuries while skiing or snowboarding. Research has shown helmets help reduce that risk by up to 60 percent.

Safety Precautions

In addition to using safety equipment, when riders hit the slopes at a resort they have to abide by certain safety rules. They are expected to pay attention to the signs of the international trail-marking system, which indicate the difficulty level of each trail on the mountain. The easiest slopes are marked with a green circle. Intermediate trails are designated by a blue square. Black diamonds warn of very difficult trails that only expert riders should attempt.

When riding at resorts, snowboarders are expected to maintain control, avoid riders and skiers downhill from them, and yield to riders and skiers coming from above.

In the international trail marking system, black diamonds indicate slopes that only expert riders should attempt.

They are expected to stop only in areas where they will be visible to others.

Unavoidable Injuries

Despite numerous safety precautions, riders sometimes get hurt while snowboarding. A 2008 study found more people were injured snowboarding than doing any other outdoor activity. The most common injuries were broken bones and sprains. About half of the injuries were caused by falling.

Falls can happen for many reasons. A rider might be off balance, hit a patch of ice, or catch an edge by digging too deeply into the snow. Tense muscles can also cause a rider to fall because they cause the rider to be less agile while moving over uneven terrain. Tense muscles can be the result of both fear and cold.

When falling, it is natural for riders to try to lessen the impact by holding out their arms. For this reason, the most common injury in snowboarding is wrist fractures. They tend to occur when riders brace themselves from a fall by putting out their arms. As their weight falls onto their wrists, the force of impact can cause a break.

"With snowboarding, everything is initiated from the core—those muscles deep within your abs and back. So when you need to get up after a fall, tighten these muscles. This is a great way to strengthen and protect your back,"[28] Gretchen Bleiler says.

Riders also crash while snowboarding. They might crash into another rider or skier if they cannot stop in time. They could crash into a tree or snowmaking equipment on the slope. Riders can avoid crashing by learning control and resting when muscles are fatigued. Looking in the direction they are going, rather than at their board helps, too. "Always look in the direction of where you want to go. If you are going downhill and someone is in your way, look to where you are headed, instead of at the other snowboarder. You'll be less likely to crash into her,"[29] Bleiler advises.

Serious Injuries

When racing and performing tricks, riders are at the most risk for serious injury. If snowboarders make a mistake at a high speed, they could crash with a dangerous force of impact. If they make a mistake in midair, they might land on their head, shoulders, or backside, which may result in a broken collarbone, concussion, or neck or shoulder injury. These kinds of injuries, particularly concussions, are

Snowboarders run the risk of serious injury as a mistake in mid-air could cause the rider to land on his head or shoulders.

common among elite snowboarders. Olympic snowboarder Elena Hight, for example, sustained about ten concussions snowboarding between ages fourteen and twenty.

A mild concussion, a brain injury caused by impact to the head, can usually be treated with rest and pain relievers. Occasionally, however, the damage is more severe. While practicing in 2009, professional snowboarder Kevin Pearce was performing a twisting double backflip when he fell and hit his head during a landing. Although he was wearing a helmet, he sustained a traumatic brain injury. He spent five months in the hospital and by mid-2010 it was too soon to tell if he would be able to return to competitive snowboarding. He did, however, hope to get back to enjoying the sport.

"The severity of Pearce's injury was unprecedented for competitive snowboarding. But hard hits to the head, including concussions, are not uncommon. As half-pipes increase in size and tricks become more technically difficult and dangerous, head injuries are becoming more prominent,"[30] writes Matt Higgins.

Long-Term Risks

Robert Cantu, a physician and professor of neurosurgery at Boston University Medical School, has found there are long-term effects to be considered, too. He conducted research about the everlasting effects of multiple concussions on snowboarders and other athletes. He and his team found an increased risk for chronic traumatic encephalopathy, a brain disease that can cause symptoms that include depression, memory loss, and dementia. The disease is degenerative, which means it gets worse over time. "The athletes are definitely more skilled than ever before. They've taken all these activities to a new level," he says. "But they've also definitely increased the risks."[31]

Top snowboarders have expressed concern about the risks they take. Most, however, accept the dangers in order to perform in their sport. "I think I can speak for everyone in saying that's just a part of what we do. We fall, get back up, and we try it again. It's the best part of our sport. You can take a crash and come back and succeed over it, and it's just the best feeling you can have,"[32] Shaun White says.

CHAPTER 4

Glides and Turns

Beginners start snowboarding for a variety of reasons. Many want to enjoy the great outdoors. Some hope to perform the impressive tricks they have seen other riders accomplish. Others want to keep up with older siblings on the slopes. Hannah Teter, for example, grew up with older brothers Abe, Elijah, and Amen, who were involved in the sport. "I watched them for a couple of years, and I would go to Abe's competitions in Vermont and see how cool [snowboarding] looked. He would build little jumps in our backyard and go flying off of them, and made it look like so much fun, so I wanted to try," she says. "I was pretty good right off the bat, because I knew the mechanics of it from watching them."[33]

Shaun White started snowboarding at age six at his mother's suggestion. He was so speedy on skis, she hoped the new sport might slow him down. "I thought, well, we'll put him on a snowboard and then he'll fall all the time and we won't have to worry about trying to dig him out of the trees," says Shaun White's mother, Cathy. "The snowboard was my safety measure."[34]

White quickly learned to go just as fast on a snowboard, however. Like all snowboarders, he learned basic skills, such as balancing, gliding, and turning. Then, he built on them to improve his performance on the slopes.

A snowboarder must learn the basic skills of balancing and turning before increasing speed and building performance skills on the slopes.

Staying in Balance

Snowboarders have to learn to control their body and their snowboard in changing—and sometimes treacherous—conditions. Balance is one of the most important basic skills in snowboarding. Staying in balance can be challenging, because snowboarders continually shift their weight as they move down a slope. For this reason, they need to develop their sense of dynamic balance, or balance in motion. People who ride already have experience with dynamic balance. It comes into play when walking, running, and performing many other physical activities.

   As author Julia Carlson explains:

Consider riding a bike: Push off so you're moving forward and it's actually pretty easy to stay balanced side-to-side. You have to lean forward ever so slightly to keep your body over the moving bike, but other than that

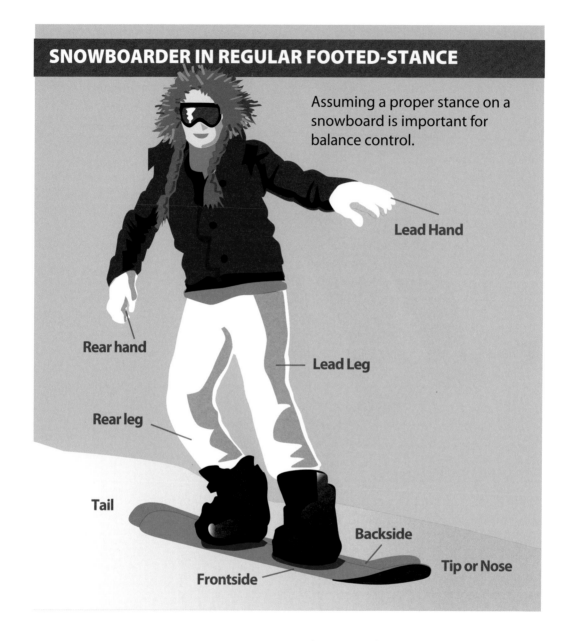

SNOWBOARDER IN REGULAR FOOTED-STANCE

Assuming a proper stance on a snowboard is important for balance control.

Lead Hand

Rear hand

Lead Leg

Rear leg

Tail

Backside

Tip or Nose

Frontside

you can pretty much coast. Of course, you also have to keep an eye out for obstacles, lean into the turns, hunker down for the bumps, and so on. Scary stuff at first, but soon it becomes second nature.... Snowboarding is amazingly similar.[35]

On a snowboard, riders use specific tactics to stay in dynamic balance. They create resistance to outside forces that could knock them off balance, such as bumps in the snow, by lining up their body's center of gravity over the center of the board. They also line up their head, shoulders, hips, and ankles vertically, in what is called a stacked position. They tighten muscles in their core and legs to create strength that will keep them upright and in control.

In addition, snowboarders create more stability by bending their knees to lower their center of gravity. This stance also enhances stability by putting added pressure on the board, pushing edges into the snow. Putting pressure on the board also melts snow as the rider moves. The fine film of melted snow under the base of the board helps reduce friction.

Gliding Along

Snowboarders start to get a feel for the board on snow by skating and gliding on flat terrain and shallow slopes. During the glide, new riders have a chance to practice dynamic balance at a low speed.

Riders skate by removing their back foot from the binding and shifting most of their weight to their front foot. They use their back foot to push off. Then, they place it on the board and put more weight on it again. When weight is evenly distributed to both feet, riders have more stability on the board.

Momentum from the push off makes the board glide over the snow. Riders make sure weight is distributed evenly between their heels and toes, so the board will stay flat. Too much pressure at either point could cause the board to tilt. They may be tempted to look down at the board, but looking straight ahead keeps their body aligned and in a stable stance.

Gaining Speed and Skills

Gliding is fine for flat terrain, but snowboarders need additional skills to handle pitches. On steeper terrain, including shallow slopes, the force of gravity pulls riders down the mountain. This puts Newton's first law of motion into action: An object in motion stays in motion unless acted

Gliding on flat terrain allows riders to practice dynamic balance at slow speeds.

upon by another force. In snowboarding, gravity's pull is strongest at the fall line, the steepest and most direct route down the slope.

As riders head down, they pick up momentum, gaining kinetic energy as they go. The faster they travel, the more difficult it is to stay in control or change direction to avoid obstacles such as trees or other riders. They can do both, however, by using their edges to create turns.

Professional snowboarder Betsy Shaw discusses the importance of learning this skill:

> Your edges are your lifeline: The more you learn how to master them, the more control you will have over your board. The more control you have over your board, the wider the variety of trails you can feel comfortable on. Also, it is important to develop a feel for the snow. As conditions vary, so must your amount of edge pressure. ... It is important to learn to adapt to your particular environment—it's all part of mastering the mountain.[36]

Mastering Edge Control

Snowboarders learn edge control by traversing. Traversing cuts a path across a hill rather than down it. By going back and forth in a zigzag pattern, snowboarders can very gradually traverse down a mountain. This pattern offers speed control, because the rider is moving perpendicular to the fall line.

To begin traversing, snowboarders angle the board slightly downward. This allows them to use the force of gravity for forward motion. They apply pressure to the board with the foot that is in front in the direction they want to move. As the board slides sideways, snowboarders use their edges to stay in control.

Traversing, or cutting a path across a hill in a zig-zag pattern, helps snowboarders to learn edge control.

Rookie Rider Mistakes

While learning to snowboard, beginners and even more experienced riders often make mistakes. One of the most common is trying to create a turn by rotating the upper body and swinging the arms around. In other circumstances, swinging the arms would help create momentum for the turn. On a snowboard, however, the action wastes energy and puts the rider off balance.

Working against gravity is another common mistake. For beginners, it may feel safer to lean back, away from the direction they are traveling. Instead, however, that stance will put the rider off balance. Fighting gravity is also less energy efficient and puts added stress on leg muscles.

When snowboarders use, or set, their edges, they carve tracks in the snow that help them create turns as well as gain traction that keeps them from slipping. They set their edges while in motion by tilting the board to apply pressure to either the heel side or the toe side. The side that receives the pressure digs into the snow.

Learning to Turn

Like traversing, turning helps riders control speed because their path cuts across the fall line. In turns, however, snowboarders tend to follow the fall line more closely. They aim to work with gravity and gain speed while maintaining control. They also have to balance against the effects of centrifugal force, which is created based on their speed and their turning radius. Centrifugal force pushes the rider out in a curved path away from the center of rotation.

Snowboarders learn skidded turns first. In skidded turns, riders use their feet to steer. First, they point the nose of the board down the fall line, apply pressure in the front foot, and move their hips forward to pick up speed. Then, they apply pressure to the back foot pressing downhill to pivot the board in a new direction. They have to be careful not to apply too much pressure, however. That could cause the board to over rotate, sending the rider sliding backward down the hill.

Carved turns are a more advanced way to turn that builds on skidded turns. In carved turns, riders focus more on using their edges, digging them into the snow for more control at higher speeds. To perform carved turns, riders use their body weight to apply pressure one side of the board to tip the board on its opposite edge. As they ride across the fall line, they switch edges by changing the side on which they apply pressure.

Riders learn basic carved turns first. In basic carved turns, hips and shoulders are kept parallel to the board. As they gain skills, riders can perform dynamic carved turns. In dynamic carved turns, hips and shoulders are parallel to the snow and the lower body does more of the work to turn.

Using their edges allows riders to put the board's sidecut and flex to work for steering. Applying pressure to set the edges bends the board so it will follow the curved shape of the sidecut. By switching edges to ride back and forth down a slope, snowboarders link turns and create a track in the snow. With experience, they can gain more control of how and where they travel.

Carlson writes:

Eventually you figure out that carving comes in varying degrees: You can push with all your might through each turn, ricocheting back and forth from one edge of the trail to the other. Or you can back off and press lightly with your edges, letting the sidecut of your board do most of the work. Either way it's about playing your weight against the board: First you tilt it up on edge, then you throw your body weight against it so it bends. The board first absorbs all that energy and then shoots it back like a slingshot, conveniently launching you into the next turn. The harder you push on the first part, the harder it snaps back at the end.[37]

Handling Terrain

While carved turns are a more advanced skill than skidded turns, experienced snowboarders do not outgrow skidded turns. No matter what their level, they use the types of turns

The Art of Stopping

Beginning riders who are not skilled in stopping often stop by sitting back onto the ground and skidding along the snow. The friction creates resistance, slowing them down until they stop.

When advanced snowboarders want to stop, they make an aggressive turn with their board. The object is to move the board so it is positioned perpendicular to the fall line. At the same time, the edge needs to be dug into the snow so the board is not flat. Riders accomplish this by putting weight in both legs and applying pressure to the uphill edge of the board.

that will help them best handle the terrain and conditions. For example, carved turns provide extra stability on a steep slope and when a rider is moving at a high rate of speed. Skidded turns are more effective when a rider is moving slower on a shallower pitch.

On any given day, and even throughout the day, the terrain and conditions on a mountain can change dramatically. A smooth slope might develop bumps after several riders have gone down. The snow might start out as powder and turn to crust or ice. Snowboarders, especially those who want to experience all-mountain snowboarding, develop their skills so they can handle whatever surprises they may encounter. Authors Jeff Bennett and Scott Downey write in *The Complete Snowboarder,* "All types of snow conditions can be ridden with similar techniques. Granted, each type of snow has a slightly different feel, but each takes only a little fine-tuning of skills you already have."[38]

Snow Conditions

Atmospheric conditions determine how snow crystals are formed and what kind of snow falls during a storm. Snow forms when water vapor freezes into ice crystals. As the crystals fall, they take on more water vapor to grow. When they reach warmer air near the Earth, they may stick together to form large flakes.

The shape of the crystals is determined by temperature and water vapor in the air. For example, star crystals form when the temperature is about 5 °F (−15 °C). Columns are denser than star crystals and form when the air is dry and temperatures are between –13° and 5°F (−25° to −15 °C). Dendrites form when the atmosphere contains high levels of water vapor, while plates form when moisture in the air is minimal. Temperatures are between −13 °F and −4°F (−25° to −20 °C).

Different kinds of crystals produce different kinds of snowboarding conditions. Many riders prefer riding powder—snow that is deep and light. Because the snow is soft, however, it is also easy to sink down into it.

Deep, light snow, known as powder, gives a rider the feeling of floating, but without enough speed the conditions make it easy for the snowboarder to sink.

SHREDDING AND STOMPING

1,140 inches (29m)

The record set for the most snowfall measured in the United States for a single season. It occurred at the Mount Baker Ski Area, in Washington State, during the 1998–99 season, according to the U.S. National Oceanic and Atmospheric Administration.

"Powder is surfing. Powder is floating. Powder can melt the distinction between ground and sky and send your board flying effortlessly through space," write Bennett and Downey. "For all of its magic, powder sometimes intimidates the unfamiliar rider. ... Think of a water skier being dragged behind a powerboat: It takes some speed before the skis plane to the surface and lift the skier above the water. The same thing happens when you're snowboarding. If you go slow, you sink. Once that happens, the snow wraps around your legs and drags you to a halt. Speed lets you plane."[39]

By keeping up speed, riders plane, or glide, over the surface of the snow. According to Randy Price, the board's design also helps because the tip turns up, lifting it out of the snow. "People often have the misunderstanding that leaning back in powder somehow makes powder riding more efficient," he says. "In truth, the idea is simply to get more of the board out of the snow and that starts at the tip. Leaning back usually just makes the board 'plow' into the snow more, slowing the board down and making it sink more."[40]

Riding on Ice

While snowboarders may love powder as a general rule, they do not usually like riding on ice. It is not easy to dig an edge into a hard surface of ice. Without strong edging, riders have less stability and are likely to slip out of control. "[Ice] magnifies your mistakes and saps your confidence,"[41] write Bennett and Downey.

"Crust" and "crud" also pose special challenges for snowboarders. Crust is snow that is hard on top and soft underneath. Snowboarders can crack through the crust as they ride, and loose, hard crust can catch their edge. Crud is heavy, chunky snow that can also trip up riders.

In both conditions, riders have to pay extra attention to the terrain. As they approach chunks of snow, they may be able to use them as jumps that will launch them slightly into the air. Making a turn in the air is easier than pushing the board through heavy snow. When riders notice a pile of heavy snow ahead, they may need to vary their turn radius to avoid it.

In their book, Bennett and Downey instruct riders on both crust and crud, telling them to "pull your knees up to free your board from the snow and make your turns in the air. Keep your turns short and bouncy. Be aggressive and attack the fall line. Most of all, keep your knees bent and your legs ready to flex or extend to compensate for ruts and bumps."[42]

Bumpy Ride

Many snowboarders seek out bumps in a mogul field. A mogul field is a slope where the terrain is bumped up. These bumps may be created by machines at a mountain resort. They can also be created when snowboarders and skiers ride in a path that pushes snow up into mounds.

To ride in moguls, snowboarders may turn in the troughs, avoiding the tops of bumps. Or, they may ride on top of the bumps. They often use a combination of approaches to get down a mogul field.

Riders feel the force of impact when they hit the front and top of a bump. They bend their knees and ankles to absorb the shock. They move their back hand forward for a stronger stance and better balance. Otherwise, they may lean back so their center of gravity is not centered over the board. They also vary their turn radius, so they will be able to turn at points where they are most comfortable in the terrain.

Snowboarders who can handle all-mountain riding have strong snowboarding skills. They are equipped to enjoy

Riding a mogul field—a slope with bumped terrain—can strengthen a snowboarder's skills.

varied terrain and conditions riding all over a mountain. The same skills that take them safely down steep slopes and icy moguls can be used to seek out new challenges. Many snowboarders also like to ride in a terrain park, a special area on a mountain that is covered with snow features like bumps, pipes, and rails, where they can perform tricks.

CHAPTER 5

Jumps and Rails

Once they have mastered basic skills, many snowboarders enjoy riding in a terrain park, where they can perform tricks on man-made snow features. In a terrain park, they may find half-pipes, jumps, and bumps, as well as rails and boxes. Half-pipes, jumps, and bumps are created by grooming snow into desired shapes and patterns. Rails and boxes are made of wood, metal, and plastic materials that a snowboarder can ride on top of, or grind.

Building a Terrain Park

While snowboarding is primarily a sport, many snowboarders enjoy riding in terrain parks for the chance to get creative and express themselves. The people who design terrain parks are also artistically inclined. They strive to challenge snowboarders creatively as well as physically.

Terrain park manager Eric Langman helped design Stratton Mountain in Vermont. He considers designing a park an art form, saying:

Art is in my blood. My whole family is involved artistically in something. My dad does some interior design, I have an aunt that's an art teacher, another makes costumes for a Broadway play. I guess I have more of a functional artistic skill that I'm glad I'm able to share with people. The mountain is my blank canvas.[43]

Wanted: Terrain Park Manager

Terrain park managers oversee terrain parks at mountain resorts. Their job responsibilities include designing parks, hiring and managing staff, and daily maintenance of the park, including grooming. People who want to work as terrain park managers study tourism in college, focusing on ski resort operations and management. Before landing her job as terrain park manager at Snowmass, Colorado, Isabelle Falardeau gained experience by volunteering at mountain resorts. In a 2004 interview with ShredBetties.com, an online magazine dedicated to female snowboarders, Falardeau said:

I started to get involved with terrain parks in Whistler [in British Columbia], where I went for a year off school. I volunteered with the Blackcomb Terrain Park crew once a week to get my pass. I loved it and decided to stay for an extra year, and got a paid position on the day crew! I later moved to Aspen [Colorado] where I worked at Buttermilk for four years before I moved to Snowmass [in 2003].

Source: *Shred Betties*, "Park Manager: Isabelle Falardeau," February 2004. http://www.shredbetties.com/riders/story/isabelle_falardeau.

Not only are the features in a terrain park man-made, often the snow is, too. Invented in the 1950s, snowmaking machines can be used to blow snow when and where it is needed. Snowmaking machines work by compressing air to break down water particles. When the machines shoot the air out of guns it expands, cooling the water particles so they form snow. This man-made snow is more dense than natural snow, so it melts more slowly.

"All park features are made from man-made snow, even out West," according to Jamie McCourt, park manager of Snowshoe Mountain Resort in West Virginia. "Man-made snow makes a better product. A little natural snow mixed in is good, but powder doesn't shape well."[44]

Surface Tricks

Some of the most basic tricks snowboarders start learning are surface tricks. While these moves do not take the rider off the ground, they require a strong stance, good balancing skills, and an ability to build speed and power.

A wheelie, for example, is performed by popping the nose of the board in the air. With the nose up, riders must balance on only the tail end of the board. Their center of gravity will not be directly over the center of the board. Riders can maintain stability and balance, however, by putting more weight on their back foot. Their back foot is centered over the tail of the board, which is flat against the snow providing a stable surface. Snowboarders can also perform wheelies by popping the tail in the air and riding the nose end of the board.

A nose-and-tail roll involves spinning 180 degrees. Riders progress to this trick from first learning to perform a wheelie. With the nose of the board popped up, the rider pivots on the tail to switch from a regular stance to a fakie stance and vice versa. In a regular stance, the left foot is forward. In a fakie, or goofy, stance, the right foot is forward. This trick helps snowboarders develop the skill to ride either way. "Most people heavily favor one side; others really can't tell until they've had a chance to try both stances,"[45] writes Julia Carlson.

A butter is another surface trick. Snowboarders perform butters by turning 360 degrees several times in a row. To start, riders gain some speed by riding straight down a hill. Then, they lift the tail slightly, balancing with more weight on the nose of the board. They apply pressure to the nose to pivot in a circle. Halfway through the spin, they press the board back onto the snow. Momentum from the spin takes them the rest of the way around to their starting position.

Lifting Off the Surface

An ollie is a basic trick that starts on the surface of the snow, but takes the rider into the air. "[Ollies] will launch you over small rocks, stumps, and other obstacles that you couldn't normally jump," write Jeff Bennett and Scott Downey. "They'll also teach you some of the moves used in more advanced freestyle and halfpipe tricks."[46]

SHREDDING AND STOMPING

60 acres (24.28ha)

The size of one of the largest terrain parks in the United States at Mountain Creek in Vernon, New Jersey.

When performing an ollie, snowboarders use the tail of their board like a spring. On a shallow slope, they point the board down to let gravity pull them forward. As they slide, they take their weight off the front foot and flex the nose of the board. At the same time, they apply pressure to the back foot. This action creates potential energy that is stored in the tail. That energy is released as kinetic energy when the board springs up.

The ollie demonstrates Newton's third law of physics, which states that for every action, there is an equal and opposite reaction. The force of the rider's foot down on the board is one action. This action determines how much potential energy is created. The equal and opposite reaction occurs next. The potential energy transforms into kinetic energy and the board pops up. The ollie uses the snowboard like a springboard to create both downward and upward forces.

While airborne, riders performing an ollie pull their knees to their chest so they are perpendicular to the ground. They keep the board centered underneath their center of gravity. This provides stability during the landing. Bending their knees helps riders absorb contact force, which is created when their feet hit the ground, as well as impact force. The mass of a snowboarder's body, the speed of the fall from the air, and gravitational acceleration all play a role in determining the measure of impact force.

Grinding on Rails and Boxes

Building on the skills learned to perform surface tricks, snowboarders are equipped to try tricks on rails, boxes, and other objects that are not made of snow. These tricks are called grinds because they involve grinding the base of the snowboard along an object.

"In the not too distant past, snowboarders looked at objects like logs and handrails as board-wreckers. Gnarly obstacles just waiting to steal away with a chunk of your P-tex base. Nowadays, snowboarders ollie up onto rails, slider bars, boxes—*anything legal and nondestructive*—then slide, spin, and dismount,"[47] write Bennett and Downey.

On a wood object, the rider will usually move slower than in snow due to friction that is created between the board and the object. Wood is absorbent. When it absorbs water and expands, the surface becomes bumpier and more resistant to motion. On a smooth metal object, the rider will move faster because metal is not absorbent.

A 50/50 grind starts out with an ollie. Riders put pressure on their back foot and load the tail of the board with potential energy. Then, they pop up using kinetic energy to get onto an object. Instead of going airborne, the

SHREDDING AND STOMPING

50/50 grind

The name of a snowboarding trick, first performed by skateboarders. It is named the 50/50 grind because for skateboarders, the trick requires grinding both axles (which hold the wheels) simultaneously.

rider performs the trick by riding, or grinding, parallel to the object along the top.

At the end of a 50/50 grind, snowboarders load the tail of their board with potential energy again. Kinetic energy launches them upward and off the object so they can land on the snow.

Building on the 50/50

A rock-and-roll grind is similar to a 50/50 grind with one major difference. Instead of riding parallel to an object, riders take a perpendicular position. The trick starts with an ollie to launch. Then, riders twist at the hips so their board lies across the object. The board needs to be centered on the object so weight is evenly distributed on each side for balance.

In a perpendicular position, the board's edges grind against the object. If the front edge catches the rail as the rider moves forward, the board will stop abruptly. Momentum keeps riders' bodies in motion, however, causing them to fall forward. In order to prevent this from happening, riders apply pressure to the heel side of the board to lift their front edge slightly as they ride.

A five-o grind is another more complicated trick, also building on the 50/50 grind. Both tricks start with an ollie and have riders grinding parallel to an object. In a five-o grind, however, riders perform a wheelie while grinding. Riders apply pressure to the nose of the board to pop the tail up. As they approach the end of the object, they redistribute their weight so more pressure goes to the tail, pressing it back down to the surface. If riders attempt to land while still in a wheelie, they will not have a strong base of support and could more easily lose balance. With the board flat, they can land on both feet. The length of the board is in contact with the snow, creating a large base of support and more stability.

Snowboarders build on their skills acquired from surface tricks to gain the confidence to try stunts on rails and other non-snow objects.

Turning in the Air

As riders gain experience grinding on objects, they can move on to more complicated tricks that require split-second timing. In 180 grinds, riders turn their board 180 degrees at the beginning and end of the trick. As riders launch into the air performing an ollie, they have to turn with precision and land to ride parallel to the object. At the end of the object, they time turning their board again, so they will land on the snow without losing balance.

Turning in the air can be disorienting, but proprioception helps riders land without missing the object or falling in the snow. Proprioception is a sense of orientation in space that can be developed through practice. As riders practice, they learn to understand feedback from nerve fibers called proprioceptors in their muscles, joints, ligaments, and tendons throughout their body, as well as in their inner ears. These proprioceptors take in information about motion and body positions and deliver it to the central nervous system.

When riders understand the feedback they receive, they do not need to depend on their sense of vision to tell them

When a snowboarder turns in the air, having a sense of orientation in space helps the rider land without falling or missing the object.

where they are in space. They can land precisely while staying in an upright position. This helps them stay in balance and complete the trick properly.

Elena Hight was a gymnast before she became a professional snowboarder. Sports trainer Harrison Bernstein believes proprioception has played a part in Hight's success at both gymnastics and snowboarding, saying:

> To be an expert gymnast or snowboarder, you must have great proprioception, and practicing on a balance beam is excellent for developing that skill. It trained [Hight] to know the dimensions of the beam, and where it is located relative to her center of gravity without looking at it. So as she practiced walking on the beam, then performing cartwheels, and eventually flips, snowboarding became a piece of cake when she got to land on the ground.[48]

Jumping

Proprioception is also helpful when snowboarders perform jumps. They need to have a sense of where their body is in space in order to hit the jump and land in an upright and stable position.

Snowboarding Slang

When snowboarders describe what they are doing in the terrain park, they do not use words in ways everyone can understand. These are some common terms and definitions:

bail: To crash land in order to stop performing a trick
bullet proof: Snow that is hard and icy
gnarly: Awesome, cool; also difficult
haul: To go fast
jib: A rail
newbie: A beginner
shred: To ride with expert skill
sick: Very good
stomp: To land well

Beginners start with small jumps off bumps in the snow and small drop-offs. As they advance, however, they can make even these small jumps look impressive by loading up potential energy and using it as kinetic energy to launch. Bigger jumps can be performed off steeper drop-offs, man-made ramps, and the half-pipe.

"Small jumps seem bigger if you spring into the air. Approach the jump compressed and pop upward as you leave the lip. This gives you some extra height and keeps your body forward and over the board,"[49] write Bennett and Downey.

When riders approach a jump, they use the same skills they learned to perform an ollie. Riders lean back to build pressure in the tail of the board. The potential energy is released as kinetic energy when they pop into the air.

Landing from a Jump

Keeping their weight evenly distributed helps a snowboarder stay in control when landing.

When snowboarders pop into the air, they also have to consider how they will land. In order to stay stable and upright, they land on both feet at the same time. This puts the board

in a position that is flat against the snow, providing a large, stable surface. They have to keep their weight evenly distributed. If too much weight winds up on the tail or nose, they will build potential energy that will send them out of control as they land.

Riders often control speed upon landing by making a turn to ride toeside. This position puts a rider's strong calf muscles to work. Riders also bend their knees and ankles to absorb the contact force and impact force when they land.

Whether jumping or doing a snowboarding trick, the landing signals the end of the performance. When asked what she loves most about snowboarding, Gretchen Bleiler mentions the landing, saying "There isn't a best part because it's all good, but I love the feeling of landing a new trick for the first time. It's the scariest feeling in the world not knowing what's about to happen, but you push on, commit and land. It's one of the most satisfying."[50]

CHAPTER **6**

Aerial Moves

While jumps off ramps and tricks on man-made objects can launch a snowboarder into the air, known as "catching big air," many riders want to go even higher. They want to go so high, they will have time to spin, flip, turn, and twist before gravity pulls them back down to earth. The half-pipe is a place where they can make that happen.

"In the case of halfpipes, air means *freedom*. Freedom to spin, flip, or grab your board as you please. Freedom to learn and perfect new tricks," write Jeff Bennett and Scott Downey. "Tricks should be an expression of your own ingenuity. … Halfpipe riding is in an endless state of evolution, with new tricks pushing aside old tricks every year."[51]

Snowboarders can catch big air in the half-pipe to perform spins that involve rotating 180 degrees, 360 degrees, 540 degrees, and even more. They perform hand grabs, where they grab onto the board, and hand plants, which require touching a hand down on the lip of the half-pipe. Inverted aerials are also performed in the half-pipe. In these tricks, snowboarders flip forward and backward in the air, without doing hand plants. The aerial tricks performed in the half-pipe are impressive, and they are getting more so every year.

"Someday, the question about half-pipe will be whether there is any higher the sport can go, any riskier it can get," writes journalist Phil Sheridan. "The man who has pushed

Indoor Snowboarding

It rarely snows in Dubai, United Arab Emirates. There is a ski resort located there, however, and snowboarders are more than welcome.

Ski Dubai is an indoor ski resort about the size of three football fields. It sits on 237 square feet (22,500 sq m). The resort includes a Freestyle Zone as well as a quarter pipe that is 295 feet (90m) long.

the envelope the most, Shaun White, won his second Olympic gold medal [in 2010] … on Cypress Mountain. … The gap between White and the other competitors was apparent even to the most novice half-pipe observers."[52]

Reaching New Heights

When performing in the half-pipe, beginner snowboarders may go about 2 feet (.6m) above the lip and into the air. That height gives them time to make a turn while airborne. Professional snowboarders go much higher, however. At the 2010 Olympic Games, Shaun White defended his title as an Olympic medalist in the half-pipe event. By his final run, he had already earned the points he needed to win again. Points are awarded based on difficulty of tricks, height achieved during tricks, the rider's style, and other factors.

When White decided to try something unusual on his last run, he was determined to prove himself and amaze the international crowd of spectators. He launched about 20 feet (6m) into the air to perform a trick he had been practicing for as long as he could remember. He spun around three and a half times and flipped twice before landing. At the time, White was the only snowboarder at his level capable of performing the trick in competition. He called it the Double McTwist 1260 because it is an embellished version of the original McTwist that was first performed in skateboarding.

In order to gain the vertical height required to perform half-pipe tricks like the Double McTwist 1260, snowboarders need

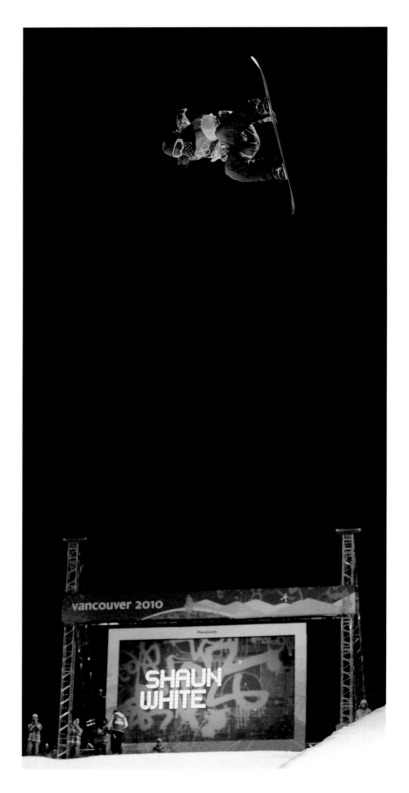

Snowboarder Shaun White performing his Double McTwist during the 2010 Olympic Games.

to put scientific forces to work. They need to build speed to punch up into the air, fighting the downward pull of gravity. They also fight against friction, which is created when an object comes in contact with air molecules and creates drag, which is a resistance to motion. Crouching at the base of the half-pipe and standing up as they approach the wall helps riders build potential energy that will be released as kinetic energy when they launch. The higher the wall, the more potential energy the rider can store.

Riding back into the base of the half-pipe, riders work with gravity to gain more speed. That speed helps them gain

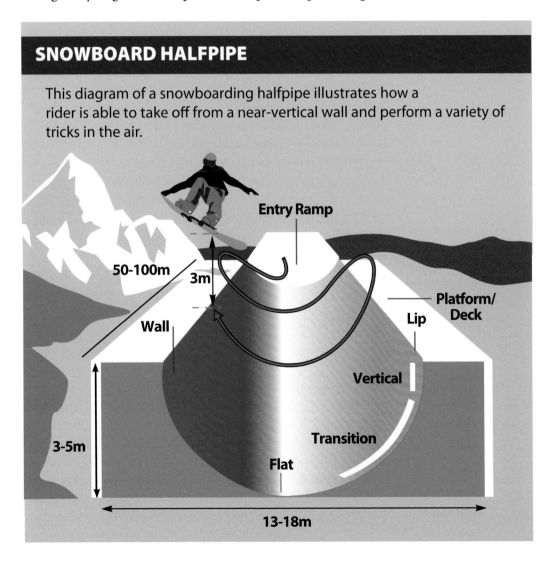

SNOWBOARD HALFPIPE

This diagram of a snowboarding halfpipe illustrates how a rider is able to take off from a near-vertical wall and perform a variety of tricks in the air.

Entry Ramp

50-100m

3m

Platform/
Deck

Wall

Lip

Vertical

3-5m

Transition

Flat

13-18m

height, but it also creates g-force. G-force is equal to the force of gravity and is created by acceleration. It pushes riders back toward the sides of the half-pipe.

"[G-force] makes you feel like you are being crushed into the wall, and the faster the boarders are going the more they have to fight back against this with strong leg, core and back muscles," writes Greg Wells. "Halfpipe snowboarders are incredible athletes. They have to have fantastic flexibility, core strength stability, muscle power, and balance."[53]

Catching Air

When snowboarders ride out of the half-pipe and into the air, they carry momentum to demonstrate Newton's first law of motion: An object in motion tends to stay in motion unless acted upon by another force. Snowboarders keep moving upward until Newton's second law of motion begins to work. Newton's second law states that the acceleration of an object is related to the force acting upon it. As snowboarders lose their momentum, gravity pushing down on them causes a change in direction. At that point, snowboarders stop moving upward and begin falling back into the half-pipe.

The higher snowboarders can get into the air, the more time they have to perform tricks. In the alley-oop, riders make a 180 degree turn in the air above the half-pipe. This is a basic half-pipe trick snowboarders need to learn before advancing to 360s, 540s, and 720s. Each is named in reference to the rotation a snowboarder makes in the air. In a 360, riders spin 360 degrees, rotating all the way around one time. In a 540, they spin 540 degrees, or one and a half times. In a 720, they spin 720 degrees, or two full rotations. Professional snowboarders can make even more rotations, such as when White performed his Double McTwist 1260.

Snowboarders also perform grabs to add style to other tricks. In a grab, riders bend their knees up toward their

SHREDDING AND STOMPING

62 feet wide (18.9m) and more than 500 feet long (152m)

The size of the Super Duper Pipe at Mammoth Mountain Ski Area, in Mammoth Lakes, California.

chest so they can grab the board while airborne. "Most grab tricks can be broken down into five-step progressions: Bring your knees up, reach down to grab the board, let go of the board, extend your legs to reach for the landing, and absorb the landing with your knees," write Bennett and Downey. "These progressions make grabs easier by bringing your board closer to your body. They also aid your balance by keeping your body compressed and centered."[54]

Special Snowboard Training

Learning complicated aerial tricks is not as easy as simply going out to the half-pipe and making an attempt. Snowboarders have to gain confidence and skills along the way, without risking injury. Many snowboarders use special equipment for training in the half-pipe. They may use a trampoline to practice jumps, flips, and spins. They may practice aerial moves over a pool of water or a pit filled with foam.

Elite snowboarders also have special opportunities for extra practice. Before the 2010 Olympic Games, White had his own private half-pipe built at Silverton Mountain ski area in Colorado. The half-pipe was 500 feet long (152m), 22 feet deep (6.7m), and was accessible only by helicopter. One section of the half-pipe was filled with foam cubes,

Backcountry Big Air

Some snowboarders seek big air on jumps they cannot access at a ski resort or by riding a chairlift. Instead, they take a helicopter to those remote locations.

Alaska's Chugach Mountains are a popular location for helicopter snowboarding. The combination of cold air from Alaska and warm air from the Pacific Ocean make the weather in the mountains perfect for producing powder. Several snowboarding movies have been filmed in the Chugach Mountains, including *Lines*, *That's It, That's All*, and *First Descent*.

Many snowboarders use special equipment, like a trampoline, to train and practice flips, jumps, and spins.

which provided padding to absorb the impact during falls. Since he knew he was not being watched by fans, White's hideaway gave him a psychological edge as he worked out new tricks. In addition, having access to a personal half-pipe meant he could practice all he wanted. "Silverton was amazing. It was a once-in-a-lifetime opportunity to work on tricks away from everyone else, to be able to take chances,"[55] White says.

Breaking Down Tricks

While White is the only snowboarder who can perform the Double McTwist successfully, even advanced tricks can be broken down so that riders can learn them. In an article for professional snowboard instructors, authors Chuck Roberts and John Roberts explain how a frontside 360 with a grab can be taught as seven separate elements. In a frontside 360, riders ride up the half-pipe, pop into the air, grab their board, and spin around 360 degrees before landing.

The approach is the first part of the trick and includes two separate elements: setup and pre-wind. During the setup, snowboarders ride up the wall of the half-pipe, taking stock of their speed. As they fight the force of gravity, their speed will decrease. Riders also make decisions during the setup about their turn shapes (whether they will carve large or small arcs in the snow), the amount of pressure they apply to their edges and their line.

Pre-wind refers to the way riders twist their upper body before a spin. "You want to be almost fully counter-rotated in the opposite direction of the spin (pre-wound) as you carve on your heel edge," Roberts and Roberts write.

> The slight edge establishes a track in the direction of the rotation and provides a stable platform from which to 'pre-wind' the upper body—that is, slightly rotate the upper body opposite the direction of rotation prior to initiating the actual spin. After pre-winding, the rider will find that the edge provides a firm foundation to push against when unwinding to create the spin.[56]

Taking Off

The next part of the trick is the takeoff. Getting it right will help the rider in other elements of the trick. This is where the rider begins to unwind while riding up the side of the half-pipe. "In unwinding, the rider unleashes rotational energy,

SHREDDING AND STOMPING
1979
The year that the first recognized snowboarding half-pipe was located in a dump in Tahoe City, California

using the edged board as a stable platform from which to spin and spring during takeoff,"[57] Roberts and Roberts write.

Riders unwind while on the snow's surface. They hold their edges in the snow so they do not begin to spin yet, however. "Early release can cause a pre-spin, in which the body rotates while the board is in contact with the snow," comment Roberts and Roberts. "This can make the rider hit the lip in a near sideslip fashion, which can diminish air time and compromise positioning while spinning."[58]

Unwinding builds pressure at the tail of the board creating potential energy. It is released as kinetic energy when riders reach the lip of the half-pipe and extend their legs to pop up into the air. Rotational energy and rotational momentum from the unwind help them continue the spin.

The takeoff is when a rider builds up pressure, creating potential energy in the tail of the board while riding up the side of the halfpipe.

By twisting their upper body in the direction of the spin, riders can increase their rotational momentum, or tendency to continue rotating.

When riders spin in a frontside 360, they rotate around the longitudinal axis. The longitudinal axis is an imaginary line that runs vertically from head to toe through a rider's body. In order to perform the frontside 360 properly, riders center their axis of rotation between their feet.

During other types of tricks, riders spin on the transverse axis and the medial axis. The transverse axis is an imaginary line that runs horizontally across a rider's waist. The medial axis is an imaginary line running from back to front through the rider's torso. Flips are performed on the transverse and medial axes.

Riders performing the frontside 360 need to make sure their axis of rotation is equally centered between bindings. Rotating the upper body creates pressure in the tail of the board. Riders release this pressure at the top of the lip of the ramp, by extending their legs to pop into the air.

Performing the Maneuver

The third part of the frontside 360 is the maneuver, or grab. Roberts and Roberts break down the maneuver to include the initial spin and the final spin. Riders grab the board during the initial spin. As they leave the ground, they bend their knees to bring the board up and grab the front on the axis of rotation with one hand. This maneuver reduces rotational inertia, the tendency of an object to resist rotating, by creating a compact shape where mass is concentrated rather than spread out. It also increases the speed, or velocity, of the spin, because compact shapes are less resistant to change.

"The front grab tends to reduce the rotational inertia of the body, increasing the spin rate in a manner similar to a figure skater who pulls in the arms in order to spin faster," Roberts and Roberts write. "It can also help add balance."[59]

Halfway through the spin, riders have rotated about 180 degrees. At this point, they are in the final spin and need to prepare for the landing. They extend their arms to spread their mass out. This increases rotational inertia and slows the spin. Riders also slow the spin by looking at fixed objects, objects that are not moving, to spot the landing. This slows the rotation of the rider's head and slows upper body rotation. During the final spin, riders release their grab and extend their legs to reach down to the ground for the landing.

Learning Landings

Like all aerial tricks, the frontside 360 with a grab ends with the landing. Roberts and Roberts describe the landing as having two elements: snow contact and riding away. When

Having an edge engaged after landing adds stability to the snowboarder and counteracts rotational momentum.

riders first make contact with the snow, contact force and impact force threaten to knock them off balance. Contact force is created when two objects, such as the rider and the snow, touch each other. Impact force is created when two objects collide. It is calculated based on mass of the falling object (in this case, the rider) and velocity, and time is also factored in. When riders land, they need to make sure their center of gravity is centered on the board. They land with the board slightly tilted so they can get an edge in the snow for stability.

Riding away starts when riders have an edge engaged. In addition to adding stability, this counteracts rotational momentum to stop the spin, according to Roberts and Roberts. When riders have their board under control, they can ride away from the half-pipe.

In competition, riders are judged on each element of the trick, including height, falls, stops, landing, and how well the trick was performed overall. Competitive snowboarders are expected to push the envelope with their tricks. "In some other sports it might be considered strange to show up doing something that's never been done before, but we definitely get rewarded for it,"[60] White says.

CHAPTER 7

Inside the Mind of a Snowboarder

Since before their sport was officially recognized by mountain resorts and major competitions, snowboarders have struggled to overcome a stereotyped image. They have been labeled fearless, reckless, and careless. They have been called athletes with an attitude. Those labels still stick today, in part because snowboarding tends to attract independent thinkers who believe in nonconformity.

Snowboarders do not always fit in with other athletes or act the way spectators expect them to act. At the Olympic Games in 2006, Lindsey Jacobellis created controversy when she attempted an unnecessary trick as she was about to win a gold medal in snowboardcross. Since she was way ahead of her competitors, she tried to grab her board during a jump. Instead of impressing the crowd, she fell and wound up in second place.

"To snowboarders, showboating isn't silly. It's snowboarding," writes journalist Jerome Solomon. "It is an interesting sport with mostly young, mostly rebellious participants. The establishment can't tell them anything."[61]

Many people were disappointed with Jacobellis for making the choice to grab the board. Jacobellis claimed afterward that she was not attempting an extra trick with the grab. She was only trying to gain stability. She did not seem to regret her decision, however, despite the way it turned out.

Japanese snowboarder Kazuhiro Kokubo (pictured in sunglasses) caused controversy in the 2010 Olympics because he appeared in public with his shirt untucked and his tie loosened.

"She later admitted she was, perhaps, trying to finish with a flourish. But the underlying message was obvious: that is what snowboarders do," writes journalist John Branch. "If there was embarrassment, it was for falling on such an easy trick."[62]

Japanese snowboarder Kazuhiro Kokubo also caused controversy before the 2010 Olympic Games. This time the problem focused on a snowboarder's appearance rather than performance. Kokubo was seen in public wearing his Olympic uniform with his tie loose, his pants hanging over his hips and his shirt untucked. When the media caught up to him, he nearly lost his chance to compete.

According to journalist Luke Winn,

Kokubo is a dreadlocked product of snowboarding culture who clashes directly with the societal expectations of old-guard Japan. There was public outcry among Japanese conservatives over Kokubo's perceived disrespect for his status as an Olympian. ... When the Ski Association of Japan [SAJ] asked him to apologize, he did so only half-heartedly in a press conference and the

SHREDDING AND STOMPING

Traditionally extreme sports have attracted mainly men in their teens and early twenties. While fewer participate, young women have proven successful in extreme sports, too.

SAJ attempted to kick him off their team due to his attitude. ... The question of how someone could get kicked off of an Olympic team for a loose tie, untucked shirt and impolite comments seems absurdly stupid when raised in the context of the sport of snowboarding. Its culture *celebrates* renegade behavior.[63]

Celebrating Snowboarders

Renegade behavior is not always punished or looked down upon in snowboarding. After all, snowboarders are also known for impressing fans and spectators with their independence, creativity, and even risky behaviors.

When Greg Dacyshyn, creative director for Burton Snowboards, designed uniforms for the 2010 U.S. Snowboarding Team, he paid tribute to the character traits that make snowboarders so unique. His aim was to design a uniform that would set the team apart from other athletes and show them as individuals even while dressed alike. "Board sports, for the most part, are about expressing individuality—that's what makes them cool,"[64] Dacyshyn says.

When showy tricks end in victory, the media are much more likely to celebrate these aspects of a snowboarder's personality. The media were excited, for example, when Shaun White performed the dangerous Double McTwist 1260 at the 2010 Olympic Games. He had already won the gold, so the trick was unnecessary. White had invented and perfected the trick, however, and he wanted to show it off. On his second run, he decided to take the risk just for the glory of the moment. "I was standing up there, I wanted a victory lap that would be remembered," he says. "I achieved that."[65]

More than Nonconformists

Snowboarders like White invent new tricks and take risks that push the sport to evolve. They also push themselves

Many riders invent new tricks and push snowboarding to evolve.

as individual athletes, using their creative abilities to keep the sport dynamic and interesting. Once they have learned, practiced, and polished a trick, they need a new move to work on. New moves keep them challenged in the sport.

Professional snowboarder Peter Line stays motivated by attempting new maneuvers. "For a while, doing the same tricks off the jumps gets really boring, you get burned down that way. So I try some new tricks in order to keep it fun, that's motivation right there,"[66] he says.

Judging new moves has become more complicated, however, as snowboarders have developed the sport. Since 1998 snowboarders have been allowed to perform moves in the Olympic Games that judges themselves have not mastered. As a result, when snowboarders try new tricks in competition, they take the risk that the judges will not be able to accurately score them.

Journalist Hannah Karp says snowboarders take psychological and physical risks when performing for judges who do not seem to understand the technical aspects of their advanced moves. She writes,

> Many top riders, including Mr. [Shaun] White, are haunted by the prospect of becoming the next Jonny Moseley, the free-spirited American mogul-skiing champion who failed to medal at Salt Lake City in 2002 despite his debut of a revolutionary trick he dubbed the "Dinner Roll." Though he executed it perfectly and the move has since elicited higher marks for difficulty, he received lower scores for his jumps at the time than his competitors got for their tried-and-true twists.[67]

Mosely scored low in part because the trick went against a rule prohibiting inverted moves at the Olympics. He performed the Dinner Roll to purposely challenge that rule. In addition, however, judges were not familiar with his trick and could not accurately score it. They had not seen it before and none of them could do the trick themselves, so they had no idea how difficult it really was to perform.

Dedicated Athletes

While snowboarders are known for taking chances to develop their sport, they are more than risk-takers, independent thinkers, and nonconformists with attitude. They are also serious athletes who are dedicated to perfecting their skills on the snow.

White, for example, has devoted his life to being the best in the sport since he began competing as a snowboarder at age seven. "His bone, body, brain and synapses [nerve impulses] make him who he is. But there are a lot of natural athletes," his coach Bud Keane says. "What sets him apart is his extreme commitment to training, to perfection. He has an uncompromising attitude toward his efforts. He works harder than anyone, and he's the most talented."[68]

Riders at every level have to put in plenty of time practicing their skills. That takes mental focus and determination. If they want to improve, they have to make the decision to practice, even in less-than-ideal weather conditions and often when they would rather be doing something else. Even for top-level snowboarders, the decisions to stick with the sport require some psychological maneuvering.

Gretchen Bleiler credits goal setting, a technique that works for many snowboarders, with helping her take charge of her time and training.

"Goals are the secret," she says. "I have at least one goal that I work toward each day. It's all about taking hold of the day, rather than letting the day run you."[69]

When they cannot meet their goals in practice, professional snowboarders may feel frustrated. Serious riders are typically psychologically strong enough, however, to stick with their long-term goal of becoming a better rider. If they are not performing well during a particular training session, they have to overcome the frustration and temptation to give up and to blame themselves.

Some riders, therefore, look to sources outside of snowboarding to help build up their confidence. Kelly Clark, for example, found she became a better rider and learned to enjoy herself more when she turned to her religion for support.

"At the end of the day, I'm not getting my self-worth [only] from how I do in the contests. As a result, it's really made my snowboarding have so much more freedom," she says. "I can really have so much more fun because [snowboarding is] not such a pressure situation. I'm just doing it because I enjoy it."[70]

SHREDDING AND STOMPING

2007

The year that snowboarding ranked as the fourth most popular extreme sport in the United States according to the Sporting Goods Manufacturers Association.

Feeling Fear

Frustration and lack of motivation are not the only obstacles snowboarders have to overcome. They also face another challenge: fear. After all, sliding down a mountain while strapped to a board is not an activity that is natural to humans. Snowboarders have to become comfortable with every aspect of the sport, including building momentum, maintaining speed, working with gravitational forces, and working against them to punch high into the air.

The amygdala is the part of the brain that experiences fear on a subconscious level and reacts, triggering the release of coritsol and other hormones. When snowboarders feel fearful, these hormones cause tense muscles, increased heart rate, and sweating. Riders often have good reason to feel afraid.

Snowboarders face the obstacle of fear as they slide down a mountain, strapped only to a board.

Extreme Snowboarding

Extreme snowboarders take excessive risks that could injure or even kill them. Some research has held that people do extreme sports because they get addicted to the physical sensations produced under stress. When extreme snowboarders do dangerous moves, stress triggers their adrenal glands to release adrenaline. This hormone causes the heart rate to increase, bringing more blood to muscles and allowing for quicker responses.

Other research, however, has found that serious athletes who do extreme sports are seeking more than danger and an adrenaline rush. They are also excited to develop courage and humility. They take calculated risks, which are well-planned in accordance with their abilities.

While they do feel afraid, "participants do not freeze with fear; instead their perceptions seem to open up, resulting in the same heightened sense of awareness and calmness associated with meditation," wrote journalist Lindsey Konkel on the Scienceline Web site in July 2009.

Source: Lindsey Konkel, "Extreme Psycholgy," *Scienceline*, July 13, 2009. http://www.scienceline.org/2009/07/health-konkel-extreme-sports-risk-psychology/.

"When I'm learning these tricks, it's a bit frightening," White says. "This year [2010], especially, pushing for the Olympics, people were getting hurt all over the place. Broken collarbones, torn rotator cuffs—friends got knocked out."[71]

Fighting Back

Riders combat fear by practicing their moves, so they know they can handle the physical side of snowboarding. They also practice specific techniques to push past their fears. Before attempting a new trick, for example, they visualize a successful performance. Continued achievement builds confidence, so they can attempt progressively more advanced tricks. Snowboarders consider their past mistakes and use good judgment, too. Sometimes, they need to have enough confidence to decide their fear is rational, such as when conditions are unsafe or they are too tired physically to perform.

"I feel like I am constantly working with fear," Bleiler says. "As a professional snowboarder, it's your job to be the best, which means that every single day you have to push past your comfort zone. Scaring yourself every day is just in the cards."[72]

Professional snowboarder Danny Davis believes riders should not even attempt a move if they are afraid, but once they do try a trick they should follow through in order to minimize injury. He says:

> One thing that I've really realized is that you've got to commit. If you're unsure about something, don't try it. If you think you're gonna freak out and open up halfway through it, don't try it. There's an even bigger commitment factor with some of these new tricks, but if you can commit you'll usually be alright. Humans are like cats: We want to land on our feet, so if you commit to what you're trying to do, gravity and instinct will take care of some of the rest. It's when you spazz out that things get dangerous.[73]

When snowboarders are trying to overcome fear, the prefrontal cortex of the brain gets involved. The prefrontal cortex is where situations are examined consciously. If the snowboarder decides there is nothing to fear after all, the prefrontal cortex will signal the amygdala to stop triggering physical reactions to fear.

Under Pressure

In addition to fear, competitive snowboarders deal with stress, also referred to as nerves or pressure. When riders compete, they put pressure on themselves and feel pressure from parents, coaches, and sponsors to do their best and to win. They contend with rivalries among teammates. Competitive snowboarding is much more stressful than riding just for fun. "Snowboarding is one thing and competing is a whole different ballgame,"[74] Olympic snowboarder Elena Hight says.

Competition can be stressful for snowboarders at any level. For new riders, the pressure is compounded because they are unfamiliar with the situation. Even top snowboarders who are accustomed to competing usually battle nerves before their performance. When Bleiler was asked, in

2007, whether she still feels nervous before competing, she answered, "Always. You'd think the more you compete, the easier it'd get. The difference between now and when I first started competing, though, is that now I know how to deal with the nerves and the pressure."[75]

Competitive snowboarders battle nerves because competition causes more stress and pressure than riding for fun.

Battling Nerves

Like fear, stress also triggers the release of hormones, including cortisol. The physical reactions that result from these hormones can hinder a snowboarder's performance. These hormones can also help, however. By increasing the heart rate, cortisol creates a burst of energy snowboarders can use. It all depends on how the snowboarder interprets the stress.

The key to dealing with nerves and pressure is different for every snowboarder. While pressure can cause less experienced riders to freeze or perform poorly, professional snowboarders try to harness their anxiety. At the 2010 Olympic Games, White's stress kept him from sleeping. At the same time, he used it as inspiration to do his best. "It's his enemy and his ally," Coach Keene says. "He's scared of it, he embraces it. It gets him up in the morning."[76]

Other athletes try to take the focus away from the anxiety they are feeling. Olympic snowboarder Louie Vito used music to cope with pressure before the competition. "Anything with a good beat can really get me in the zone, but be relaxing at the same time,"[77] he says.

According to sports psychologist Shane Murphy, athletes perform best under pressure when they have a set of psychological skills to tap into under pressure. Members of the U.S. Olympic Snowboard Team worked with sports psychologists to learn those kinds of skills.

Murphy says:

Being in the "zone" isn't about perfection as much as it is about staying in the moment, not worrying about failure, and not worrying about what the result might be. I find every athlete to be unique in their approach to that "zone," but they use some combination of psychological skills such as visualization, goal-setting, concentration, relaxation or mindfulness, psyching up, positive self-talk and developing a consistent routine in order to get there. Once they're ready, they focus and let it happen. Their bodies are prepared to succeed—usually it's the mind that can get in the way—if you let it.[78]

Learning to cope with pressure in competition does not happen overnight. Snowboarders train mentally as well as physically during all the years in which they compete in the sport. There is no exact science, and what works for one athlete may not work for another. In the end, however, they find all sorts of different ways to cope with the pressure of competing and perform to the best of their abilities.

Psychologist Kate F. Hays specializes in sports psychology and has studied how Olympic athletes deal with pressure. She explains:

Every Olympic competitor faces pressure, extraordinary pressure. They've been practicing and fine-tuning their

Bad Press Stress

Professional snowboarders face more pressure than amateur snowboarders in part because they are subject to media scrutiny. Snowboarder Gretchen Bleiler, for example, dealt with that pressure when reporters asked her how she felt just before an Olympic half-pipe competition in 2006. She answered honestly that she had never felt more nervous. When the media wrote she suffered panic attacks on the slopes, Bleiler felt she had to speak out to counter that claim.

In a November 8, 2006, story in the *Aspen (CO) Times*, she said, "Some athletes just choose to lie and say the Olympics is no big thing, that it's just another contest. That wasn't me. But then all the sudden it's 'Gretchen Bleiler is prone to anxiety.' Truthfully, I've never had a panic attack in my life."

Bleiler won a silver medal at the 2006 Olympic Games, and according to at least one journalist, Nate Peterson, she continued to talk honestly about her experiences on the slopes.

Source: Nate Peterson, "The Progression of Gretchen Bleiler," *The Aspen Times*, November 8, 2006. http://www.aspentimes.com/article/20061108/SPORTS/61107010.

physical skills for years. To have reached this pinnacle, they've also practiced and fine-tuned their mental skills. And of course the physical and mental skills interact all the time, even when we don't have good language to describe this seamless and continuous interaction between mind and body. These athletes have figured out what works best for them, in order to manage, control, and deal with pressure.[79]

Psychological Benefits of Snowboarding

Most athletes have to cope with fear and stress. Snowboarders, however, have to handle additional challenges. When they train, perform, and compete, they are scrutinized and stereotyped. Snowboarders at every level are charged with proving themselves as serious athletes while remaining true to their individuality and nonconformist ideals.

The benefits of snowboarding make it all worthwhile to those who enjoy the sport. For some, winning in a competition is the ultimate payoff. For others, the biggest advantage comes from the brain's reaction to physical

Snowboarding can trigger endorphins, which can reduce the brain's perception of pain and create an overall feeling of happiness.

exertion. Snowboarding triggers the release of endorphins, neurotransmitters in the pituitary gland and throughout the nervous system. They reduce the brain's perception of pain and create an overall feeling of well-being.

Many professional snowboarders enjoy traveling in order to train and compete. For snowboarders at every level, the sport is about self-expression, challenge, and just having fun in the snow.

"The people who take it [snowboarding] too serious or sporty don't have as much fun as the true shredders and the originators did," Olympic snowboarder Danny Kass says. "It has taught me to be open to the world around me, and has opened up many different cultures and lifestyles, and it has taught me the meaning of life, but you have to find that one out for yourself."[80]

Chapter 1: The Evolution of Snowboarding as a Sport

1. Patrick Sweeney, "Skier vs. Snowboarder Animosity Lessening," *The Denver Business Journal,*December 21, 2001. http://denver.bizjournals.com/denver/stories/2001/12/24/focus2.html

2. Video, www.wtfoodge.com, February 21, 2010.

3. John Fry, "Not That Rad," *Ski,* March/April 2010, page 27.

4. Zoe Oksanen, "I Am Burton," *Huck Magazine.* www.huckmagazine.com/features/i-am-burton/.

5. Quoted in Oksanen, "I Am Burton."

6. Roger Brooks, "Success Stories: Jake Burton Charts a New Course in Snowboarding," *Success Magazine.* www.successmagazine.com/success-stories-jake-burton-charts-a-new-course-in-snowboarding/PARAMS/article/951.

7. Bruce Horovitz, "Jake Burton Puts His Personal Stamp on Burton Snowboards," *USA Today,* February 17, 2010. www.usatoday.com/money/companies/management/2010-02-08-burton08_ST_N.htm.

8. Interview, Randy Price, American Association of Snowboard Instructors (AASI) level 3 instructor, team alum, and past AASI team coach.

9. Greg Wells, "The Science of Halfpipe Snowboard." www.drgregwells.com/wells-blog/2010/2/9/the-science-of-halfpipe-snowboard.html.

10. Interview, Randy Price.

11. Quoted in Sweeney, "Skier vs. Snowboarder Animosity Lessening."

12. Reed Albergotti, "Lots of Air, No Drama as Shaun White Takes Gold," *Wall Street Journal*, February 19, 2010. www.online.wsj.com/article/SB10001424052748703444804575072363046190100.html.

Chapter 2: Training and Conditioning for Snowboarding

13. John Branch, "Never Too Cool for a Hard Workout," *The New York Times*, February 17, 2010. www.nytimes.com/2010/02/18/fashion/18fitness.html, page 1.

14. Amy Van Deusen, "Kelly Clark," *Women's Health Magazine.* www.womenshealthmag.com/fitness/snowboarding-1, p. 1.

15. Quoted in Branch, "Never Too Cool for a Hard Workout," p. 1.

16. Sean Gregory, "Shaun White vs. Lindsey Vonn: Who's Better?" *Time*, February 18, 2010. www.time.com/time/world/article/0,8599,1964914,00.html#ixzz0iMTI0YhX.

17. Ken Galloway, "Fitness Interview with Shaun White," *Men's Health*, FoxNews.com, March 8, 2010. www.foxnews.com/story/0,2933,588385,00.html

18. Quoted in Galloway, "Fitness Interview with Shaun White."

19. Matt Higgins, "In an Olympic Year, Snowboarders Can't Wait for Winter," *The New York Times*, July 28, 2009. www.nytimes.com/2009/07/29/sports/29xgames.html.

20. Quoted in Higgins, "In an Olympic Year, Snowboarders Can't Wait for Winter."

21. "Spring Training: A Day in the Life of Graham Watanabe," U.S. Snowboarding, May 19, 2008. http://www.ussnowboarding.com/news?storyId=1194.

22. Quoted in Van Deusen, "Kelly Clark," p. 1.

23. Quoted in Branch, "Never Too Cool for a Hard Workout," p. 2.

24. Sal Ruibal, "Secret Pipe Dream Gives Shaun White a Snowboarding Edge," *USA Today*, February 9, 2010. www.usatoday.com/sports/olympics/vancouver/snowboarding/2010-02-09-shaun-white_N.htm.

25. Quoted in Van Deusen, "Kelly Clark," p. 2.

26. Lindsey Jacobellis, "How Lindsey Jacobellis Stays Calm Before the Olympics," Health.com. www.living.health.com/2010/02/04/lindsey-jacobellis-stays-calm/.

Chapter 3: Preparing for Snowboarding

27. "Hannah Teter's Tips for Buying Snowboard Gear," Owl.com, December 7, 2009. www.owl.com/article/2009/12/07/hannah-teters-tips-for-buying-snow-board-gear.

28. Loren Chidoni. "Q & A with Olympic Snowboarder Gretchen Bleiler," *Women's Health*. www.active.com/actionsports/Articles/Interview-With-Olympic-Snow-boarder-Gretchen-Bleiler.htm?act=EMC.

29. Quoted in Chidoni, "Q & A with Olympic Snowboarder Gretchen Bleiler."

30. Matt Higgins, "As Snowboarders Soar, So Does Concern," *The New York Times*, March 18, 2010. www.nytimes.com/2010/03/19/sports/19snowboard.html.

31. Higgins, "As Snowboarders Soar, So Does Concern."

32. Will Graves, "Snowboarder Shaun White Gets Creative — At Great Risk," *The Philadelphia Inquirer*, February 17, 2010. www.philly.com/inquirer/sports/20100217_Onward_and_upward.html.

Chapter 4: Glides and Turns

33. Luke Winn, "Q&A with U.S. Snowboarder Hannah Teter," SI.com. http://sportsillustrated.cnn.com/olympics/2010/blog/2010/02/23/qa-with-u-s-snowboarder-hannah-teter/.
34. Charlie English, "Shaun White: The Snowboarder's New Tricks," *The Guardian*, February 16, 2010. www.guardian.co.uk/sport/2010/feb/16/shaun-white-snowboarders-new-tricks.
35. Julia Carlson, *Snowboarding*. Camden, ME: Ragged Mountain, 1999, p. 56.
36. Carlson, *Snowboarding*, p. 66.
37. Carlson, *Snowboarding*, p. 129.
38. Jeff Bennett and Scott Downey, *The Complete Snowboarder*. Camden, ME: Ragged Mountain, 1994, p. 59.
39. Bennett and Downey, *The Complete Snowboarder*, p. 60.
40. Interview, Randy Price. July 2010.
41. Bennett and Downey, *The Complete Snowboarder*, p. 62.
42. Bennett and Downey, *The Complete Snowboarder*, p. 63.

Chapter 5: Jumps and Rails

43. "Q&A with New Terrain Parks Manager Eric Langman." Stratton Mountain, VT. www.stratton.com/mediaroom/091102_q_and_a_with_new_parks_manager.htm.
44. Roanoke Outside blog. December 1, 2009. www.roanokeoutside.word-press.com/2009/12/01/small-resort-terrain-parks-in-the-southeast-are-shredding-the-competition/.
45. Carlson, *Snowboarding*, p. 30.
46. Bennett and Downey, *The Complete Snowboarder*, p. 78.
47. Bennett and Downey, *The Complete Snowboarder*, p. 83.
48. Olympic Pulse blog, NBC Olympics, February 18, 2010. www.nbc-olympics.com/olympicpulse/blogs/blog=olympichealthandfitness/postid—427494.html.
49. Bennett and Downey, *The Complete Snowboarder*, p. 69.
50. Gretchen Bleiler. www.snowboarding.com/snowboarder/Gretchen+Bleiler.

Chapter 6: Aerial Moves

51. Bennett and Downey, *The Complete Snowboarder*, pp. 90–91.
52. Phil Sheridan, "Shaun White Soars to Half-Pipe Gold," *The Philadelphia Inquirer*, February 18, 2010. www.philly.com/inquirer/sports/20100218_Shaun_White_soars_to_half-pipe_gold.html
53. Wells, "The Science of Halfpipe Snowboard."
54. Bennett and Downey, *The Complete Snowboarder*, p. 92.
55. Sal Ruibal, "Marketing Mogul Shaun White Seeks More Gold," *USA Today*, January 28, 2010. www.usatoday.com/sports/olympics/vancouver/snowboarding/2010-01-26-white-mogul_N.htm.

56. Chuck Roberts and John Roberts, "Tune Up Those Frontside Air 360s," *32 Degrees*, Winter 2009, pp. 33 and 32.

57. Roberts and Roberts, "Tune Up Those Frontside Air 360s," p. 33.

58. Roberts and Roberts, "Tune Up Those Frontside Air 360s," p. 36.

59. Roberts and Roberts, "Tune Up Those Frontside Air 360s," p. 34.

60. *The New York Times* video. www.nytimes.com/interactive/ sports/olympics/2010-snowboard -interviews.html#/1/5.

Chapter 7: Inside the Mind of a Snowboarder

61. Jerome Solomon, "Jacobellis Lives By Boarders' Daredevil Code," *The Houston Chronicle*, February 16, 2010. www.chron.com/disp/story .mpl/sports/oly/6868733.html.

62. John Branch, "Redemption, but Not for Jacobellis," *The New York Times*, February 16, 2010. www .nytimes.com/2010/02/17/sports/ olympics/17snowboard.html.

63. Luke Winn, "Japan's 'Bad-Boy Snowboarder,'" SI.com, February 18, 2010. http://sportsillustrated.cnn.com/ olympics/2010/blog/2010/02/18/ the-kokubo-controversy/.

64. Andrew Keh, "Rings," *The New York Times* blog, December 4, 2009. www.vancouver2010.blogs .nytimes.com/2009/12/04/burton -introduces-anti-uniform-for-us -snowboarders/.

65. "Shaun White Retains Winter Olympic Halfpipe Title and Adds a Flourish," Guardian.co.uk, February 18, 2010. www.guardian.co.uk/ sport/2010/feb/18/shaun-white -halfpipe-winter-olympics.

66. Phil Orlins and Chris Gunnarson. "Q&A with Peter Line," 2000 Winter X Games. www.espn.go.com/extreme/ winterx00/s/peterlinefeature.html.

67. Hannah Karp, "When Snowboarders Baffle the Judges," *The Wall Street Journal*, November 18, 2009. www.online.wsj.com/article/SB100 01424052748704431804574541711 988394566.html.

68. Sal Ruibal, "Secret Pipe Dream Gives Shaun White a Snowboarding Edge," *USA Today*, February 9, 2010. www .usatoday.com/sports/olympics/ vancouver/snowboarding/2010-02 -09-shaun-white_N.htm.

69. Quoted in Chidoni, "Q & A with Olympic Snowboarder Gretchen Bleiler."

70. Vicki Michaelis, "'02 Halfpipe Winner Kelly Clark Keeps Feet on Ground," *USA Today*, February 10, 2010. http://www.usatoday.com/ sports/olympics/vancouver/snow -boarding/2010-02-04-clark-half -pipe_N.htm.

71. Max J. Dickstein, "Q&A Snowboard Impresario Shaun White's Olympic Victory Lap Rolls On," *AM New York*, February 25, 2010. www.amny.com/ urbanite-1.812039/q-a-snowboard -impresario-shaun-white-s-olympic -victory-lap-rolls-on-1.1781051.

72. "Three Days with Gretchen Bleiler at Home in Aspen," Transworld Snowboarding.com, October 10, 2007. www.snowboarding.transworld.net/1000026549/photos/three-days-with-gretchen-bleiler-at-home-in-aspen/.

73. Colin Bane, "Q&A: Danny Davis, Dew Tour Superpipe Champ," Denver Westword blog. December 21, 2009.

74. Go211.com—US Snowboarders Talk About the Olympic Pressure, February 22, 2010. www.vids.myspace.com/index.cfm?fuseaction=vids.individual&videoid=103162747.

75. "Three Days with Gretchen Bleiler at Home in Aspen."

76. Austin Murphy, "Using Pressure as Fuel, White Takes Place Among Rare Champions," SI.com. February 18, 2010. www.sportsillustrated.cnn.com/2010/olympics/2010/writers/austin_murphy/02/18/shaun-white/?cnn=yes&hpt=T3.

77. Louie Vito, "iPod & Xbox 360 Settle Nerves," Olympic blog, People.com, February 16, 2010. www.people.com/people/article/0,,20344517,00.html.

78. "What It Takes to be an Olympic Athlete," The American Psychological Association. February 19, 2010. www.apa.org/news/press/releases/2010/02/olympic-athlete.aspx.

79. Kate F. Hays, Ph.D., "The Edge: Peak Performance Psychology," *Psychology Today*, February 14, 2010. www.psychologytoday.com/blog/the-edge-peak-performance-psychology/201002/the-edge-coping-under-pressure.

80. "Rider Profile: Danny Kass," *Snowboarder Magazine*. www.snowboarder-mag.com/features/riderprofiles/dannykass/#http://snowboardermag.com/features/riderprofiles/danny-kass.jpg.

acceleration: An increasing rate of speed.

composite: A building material made from a variety of different ingredients.

degenerative: A condition that causes gradual loss of function.

graphics: Artistic designs.

terrain: Ground or surface.

pitch: The slant of a slope.

prototype: A first model of something to be manufactured.

sprint: A high-speed, short run.

velocity: Speed with direction.

viscous: Thick, sticky and resistant to flow.

FOR MORE INFORMATION

Books

Tina Basich, *Pretty Good for a Girl: The Autobiography of a Snowboarding Pioneer,* New York: It Books, 2003. Tina Basich started snowboarding in 1986 when the sport was new. At the 1998 Winter X Games, she became the first woman to successfully land a backside 720 in competition.

Matt Doeden, *Shaun White*. Minneapolis: Lerner, 2006. This book is a biography of Olympic snowboarder Shaun White.

Frank Gille and René Marks, *Snowboarding, Make a Perfect Start.*Oxford, UK: Meyer & Meyer Sport, 2000. This book details the history of snowboarding and explains how to perform in the sport.

Claire O'Neal, *Lindsey Jacobellis: World Class Snowboarder*. Hockessin, DE, Mitchell Lane, 2008. This book is a biography of Olympic snowboarder Lindsey Jacobellis.

Blaine Wiseman, *Snowboarding*. New York: Weigl, 2008. This book includes information about extreme snowboarding tricks as well as history, rules of the sport, and exciting moments.

Internet Sources

Tracy Anderson, "2010 Olympic Snowboard (Anti) Uniforms," ESPN Action Sports, December 7, 2009. http://espn.go.com/action/snowboarding/blog/_/post/4722162.

Isabelle Falardeau. ShredBetties. February 2004. www.shredbetties.com/riders/story/isabelle_falardeau.

Linda Holmes, "Redemption, Heartbreak, and Hot-Dogging: The Tale of Lindsey Jacobellis," NPR.com, February 17, 2010. www.npr.org/blogs/monkeysee/2010/02/redemption_heartbreak_and_hotd.html.

Lindsey Konkel, "Extreme Psychology," Scienceline. July 13, 2009, p. 3. www.scienceline.org/2009/07/13/health-konkel-extreme-sports-risk-psychology/.

Laurel Pantin, "Chatting with Olympic Snowboarder Lindsey Jacobellis, Teen Vogue, November 5, 2009. www.teenvogue.com/beauty/blogs/beauty/2009/11/chatting-with-olympic-snow-boarder-lindsey-jabobellis.html.

Nate Peterson, "The Progression of Gretchen Bleiler," *The Aspen (CO)*

Times, November 8, 2006. www
.aspentimes.com/article/20061108/
SPORTS/61107010.

ScienceDaily.com, "Helmets Must Be
Part of Skiing and Snowboarding
Culture, Doctors Urge," February
18, 2010. www.sciencedaily.com/
releases/2010/02/100217114636
.htm.

Swiss Valley Ski and Snowboard Area,
"Science of Snowboarding," www
.skiswissvalley.com/?page_id=332.

Luke Winn, "Q&A with U.S. Snowboarder Hannah Teter" SI.com, February
23, 2010. http://sportsillustrated.cnn
.com/Olympics/2010/02/23/qa-with
-u-s-snowboarder-hannah-teter/.

Web Sites

**Snowboard: Vancouver 2010 Winter
Olympics** (www.vancouver2010
.com/olympic-snowboard). This Web
site provides articles and information
about the Games and the athletes
who competed.

**USASA: United States of America Snow-
board Association** (www.usasa.org).
This organization oversees competitive
snowboarding in the United States.

**USSA: United States Ski and Snowboard
Association** (www.ussa.org). This organization is a governing body for Olympic skiing and snowboarding. The site
provides news and other information.

INDEX

PICTURE CREDITS

ABOUT THE AUTHOR

Heather E. Schwartz writes about sports, science and other interesting topics from her home in upstate New York. She enjoys skiing each winter and plans to try snowboarding the next time she is feeling brave. She lives with her husband, Philip, and son, Nolan.